ISBN 978-1-5277-4548-3
PIBN 10886875

This book is a reproduction of an important historical work. Forgotten Books uses
state-of-the-art technology to digitally reconstruct the work, preserving the original format
whilst repairing imperfections present in the aged copy. In rare cases, an imperfection in
the original, such as a blemish or missing page, may be replicated in our edition. We do,
however, repair the vast majority of imperfections successfully; any imperfections that
remain are intentionally left to preserve the state of such historical works.

1 MONTH OF
FREE
READING

at
www.ForgottenBooks.com

By purchasing this book you are eligible for one month membership to ForgottenBooks.com, giving you unlimited access to our entire collection of over 1,000,000 titles via our web site and mobile apps.

To claim your free month visit: www.forgottenbooks.com/free886875

English
Français
Deutsche
Italiano
Español
Português

www.forgottenbooks.com

Mythology Photography **Fiction**
Fishing Christianity **Art** Cooking
Essays Buddhism Freemasonry
Medicine **Biology** Music **Ancient**
Egypt Evolution Carpentry Physics
Dance Geology **Mathematics** Fitness
Shakespeare **Folklore** Yoga Marketing
Confidence Immortality Biographies
Poetry **Psychology** Witchcraft
Electronics Chemistry History **Law**
Accounting **Philosophy** Anthropology
Alchemy Drama Quantum Mechanics
Atheism Sexual Health **Ancient History**
Entrepreneurship Languages Sport
Paleontology Needlework Islam
Metaphysics Investment Archaeology
Parenting Statistics Criminology
Motivational

FACTS AND FIGURES OF THE BELFAST POGROM, 1920-1922

FACTS & FIGURES

OF THE

BELFAST POGROM
1920-1922

BY

G. B. KENNA

DUBLIN:

THE O'CONNELL PUBLISHING COMPANY

1922

TO

The many Ulster Protestants,

who have always lived in peace and friendliness

with their Catholic neighbours,

This little Book

Dealing with the Acts

of their misguided Co-religionists,

Is affectionately dedicated.

FOREWORD

THE object of this little volume is to place before the public a brief review of the disorders that have made the name of Belfast notorious for the past two years. A well-financed Press propaganda, clever and unscrupulous, taking advantage of the disturbed state of the public mind and the proverbial shortness of the public memory, has already succeeded in convincing vast numbers of people, especially in England, that the victims were the persecutors—that Abel killed Cain. The incredible has indeed been accomplished. Those vast sums have not been spent in vain.

It would be folly to hope that any dissemination of the truth can ever undo the effects of such propaganda. But it is surely due to the poor, suffering minority in Belfast that some effort should be made to put a fair statement of their case before the outside public. An honest effort is made to do this briefly here.

This book is compiled mainly from first-hand knowledge, but there is hardly anything in it which one may not verify from current reports in the unprejudiced Irish or British Press.

. What the Catholics of Belfast would desire most of all, and what they have repeatedly asked for, is an impartial tribunal set up by Government to investigate the whole tragic business. Sir James Craig's Government would never consent to do that. Would it be too much to hope that—considering the magnitude of these outrages, and the helpless civic condition of the Catholic minority—an International Commission should be appointed to take it in hand, such as was set up for an inquiry into the Turkish outrages in Anatolia?

1st August, 1922.

CONTENTS

Introduction 7

First Outbreak, 21st July, 1920 13

Are the Belfast Pogroms Anti-Catholic or Anti-National?—Omens of Peace—What a Bogus Trade Union did—The Fiery Cross—The Orange Press takes up the Cry—Coming Events—The Day Arrives (21st July, 1920)—Loyalists All—Out of the Frying Pan—Works of the Second Day (22nd July, 1920)—Storming a Church—What a British Officer saw—Firing on a Monastery—And what a Jury thought of it—Orange Braves Attack Convent of Nuns—What Officers of the Crown said about it—What an Orange Paper said about it—A Monstrous Lying Press—Quite Hamaresque—What some Outsiders had to say—English Fair Play—A Lull—Some Words of a Bishop—And of a Belfast Protestant—And a Word of Premier Craig—The Victims.

Second Outbreak, 24th August, 1920 33

One Week's Burnings—Anti-Catholic Campaign—Væ Victis—Attempt to burn a Child—Keeping the Ring—Evictions—Curfew—An Attack on a Church—Fleeing with a Corpse—What Ananias said—What a Jury said—A Judge's Remarks—Grieved by Belfast Perjury—Wanted a Victim—What the Minority are up against—The Odds—The Orange Version—Let the Truth be Known Everywhere—The Orange Special Police—The Times Disapproves—The Government Surrenders to Carson—The Times and Daily Mail—Sinning Against the Light—The Boycott.

Second Year, 1921—A Summary 57

Murder by Crown Forces—Monthly Events—Outposts Under Siege—One Against Ten—A Boy's Agony—Kicked to Death—A Cry at Westminster—How Curfew was Carried Out—"Catholics Themselves to Blame for Pogrom '!—This Picture—And This—The National Sentiment,

Wickham Secret Circular 83

The Plot Exposed—Sequence of Events—Detailed Analysis.

Samples of Orange Loyalty 92

Kicking the King's Uniform—A Letter from the King—British Soldiers Killed and Wounded.

Third Year—Law and Order Under the Belfast Parliament 95

The " Boys "—Their Qualifications—Sir James Craig Still Asks for More.

The Machine at Work 98

Babies Shot—And a Soldier of the King—"Catholic Aggressiveness"—The Collins-Craig Pact and Its Fate—Boycott of Belfast Removed—Sir James Craig Fails to Make Good—Children Slaughtered by Bomb—A Deaf Mute—How a Boy was Murdered—The Old Story—Commonplaces—Camouflaged Approval—A Timid Admission—For Protestantism—His Master's Voice—How Defenders of Empire were Treated—Law No Deterrent—Crying in Wilderness—Failure of Pact.

(5)

6   CONTENTS

INTRODUCTION

THIS book ought to be read in conjunction with some reputable history* of the Orange Order. Then it would be found that little in the following narrative is really new ; that the recent eruption in N.E. Ulster is but the latest, and most violent, perhaps, of a long series, the same in kind if differing in degree, which have blotched the story of that faction for well over a hundred years.

We might refer the reader to the third and fourth volumes of Lecky's *History of Ireland in the Nineteenth Century* for much valuable information about the early days of Orangeism. Lecky as a Unionist and a Protestant had considerable sympathy with the Order which shows itself unmistakably in some of his pages, but, as an historian, he makes, on the whole, a laudable effort to set forth the facts fairly.

As everybody knows, the Orange Society came into being on the evening following the '' battle '' of the Diamond in County Armagh, 20th September, 1795, when the assembled Peep o' Day Boys took the new name of Orangemen. And then—

---

* *The Orange Order*, by Rev. H. W. Cleary (now Bishop of Auckland), London, 1899, could hardly be surpassed as a well-written and thoroughly documented book, dealing with the subject from a Catholic point of view.

" A terrible persecution of the Catholics immediately followed," says Lecky (vol. iii., p. 429).
" The animosities between the two religions, which
had long been little bridled, burst out afresh, and,
after the battle of the Diamond, the Protestant
rabble of the county of Armagh, and of part of the
adjoining counties, determined by continuous outrages to drive the Catholics from the country.
Their cabins were placarded, or, as it was termed,
'papered' with the words, 'To hell or Connaught,'
and, if the occupants did not at once abandon them,
they were attacked at night by an armed mob.
The webs and looms of the poor Catholic weavers
were cut and destroyed. Every article of furniture was shattered or burnt. The houses were
often set on fire, and the inmates were driven homeless into the world. The rioters met with scarcely
any resistance or disturbance. Twelve or fourteen
houses were sometimes wrecked in a single night.
Several Catholic chapels were burnt, and the persecution which began in Armagh soon extended over
a wide area in the counties of Tyrone, Down,
Antrim, and Derry."

Thus was Orangeism cradled in what we now
call Pogrom.

" On December 28," continues Lecky (*ibidem*),
" about three months after the battle of the
Diamond, the Earl of Gosford, who was governor
of the county of Armagh, and a large number of
magistrates of great property and influence met at
Armagh to consider the state of the country. With

a single exception, they were all Protestants, and among them were three clergymen of the Established Church who were afterwards raised to the bench. The opening speech of Lord Gosford has often been quoted, and it furnishes the clearest and most decisive evidence of the magnitude of the persecution.

"' It is no secret,' he said, ' that a persecution, accompanied with all the circumstances of ferocious cruelty which have in all ages distinguished that dreadful calamity, is now raging in this county. Neither age, nor even acknowledged innocence as to the late disturbances, is sufficient to excite mercy, much less afford protection. The only crime with which the wretched objects of this persecution are charged is a crime of easy proof. *It is simply a profession of the Roman Catholic faith.* A lawless banditti have constituted themselves judges of this species of delinquency, and the sentence they pronounced is equally concise and terrible : it is nothing less than a confiscation of all property, and immediate banishment. It would be extremely painful, and surely unnecessary, to detail the horrors that attended the execution of so wide and tremendous a proscription, which certainly exceeds, in the comparative number of those it consigns to ruin and misery, every example that ancient and modern history can afford. For where have we heard, ot in what history of human cruelties have we read, of more than half the inhabitants of a populous country deprived at one

blow of the means, as well as of the fruits, of their
industry, and driven, in the midst of an inclement
winter, to seek shelter for themselves and their
helpless families where chance may guide them? This is no exaggeration of the horrid scenes now
acting in this county . . . . and acting with
impunity. The spirit of impartial justice (without
which law is nothing better than a tyranny) has for
a time disappeared in this county, and the supine-
ness of the magistracy is a topic of conversation
in every corner of the kingdom.'

" This terrible picture," the historian continues, " appears to have been fully acquiesced in
by the assembled gentlemen."

Pitt did not hesitate, within a few months, to
enrol this " lawless banditti " almost *en masse* in
yeomanry corps and employ them, armed and
quartered on the people, to goad the country into
a rebellion which they afterwards helped to suppress
by methods of unspeakable infamy. In like
manner, only a few months after the outbreak of
the latest Belfast pogrom we have the lawless
banditti of the shipyards, the street corners, and
quarters claiming higher respectability, gathered in
tens of thousands into a special police force, by
British authority, and empowered to trample almost
as they please upon a crushed and hated minority.

If Orangeism in its infancy was such as above
described—and no one has ever dared to contro-
vert this historical indictment—we need not marvel
at the excesses which have accompanied its growth

and development. Let those who imagine that in later years it might have become possessed by a new and better spirit read the reports of the two Parliamentary Select Committees of Enquiry into the Orange Society in 1835 which led to an Act of Parliament suppressing the Order on account of its general ruffianism and disloyalty.

Or let them read the report of an Enquiry into the happenings at Dolly's Brae in 1849, in which Mr. Walter Berwick, Q.C., Chairman of the Commission, describes the work of about three thousand armed Orangemen "as reflecting the deepest disgrace on all by whom it was perpetrated or encouraged."

Or let them take Reports of the Royal Commissions of Enquiry into the disturbances at Belfast in 1857, in 1864, and 1886, where the same tale of barbarous intolerance is told by many witnesses, chiefly Protestant. From such official reports and from dozens of eminent non-Catholic writers the Orange Society is condemned as no existing organisation we know of has been condemned.

It is exceedingly pleasant and encouraging to reflect that, notwithstanding the blighting works of this antiquated and politically-manœuvred organisation, the great masses of Catholics and Protestants in Ulster have always as a rule lived and worked together in a fine spirit of tolerance and mutual kindliness. In at least five cases out of six the Protestant will say of the Catholics, and the Catholic will say of the Protestants, " I wouldn't ask for a better neighbour." They may see little faults in each other, no doubt, but their friendship and respect for each other is as genuine as anything else the writer knows in this world.

There are many thousands of Protestants in Ulster who would thrill with horror and indignation at the true story of what has happened in Belfast and other places in the North-East. But they have not heard the truth, and their Press will see to it that, so long as it suits a political game, they shall not hear the truth.

And therein is tragedy.

BELFAST POGROM, 1920

[The reader is invited to examine the Introduction.]

FIRST OUTBREAK
21st July, 1920

ARE THE BELFAST POGROMS ANTI-CATHOLIC OR ANTI-NATIONAL?

THIS is a question often asked and seldom satisfactorily answered. The truth would seem to be that in so far as they are inspired by certain people in England* the aim is chiefly anti-National. The capitalist encourages them as being anti-Trade Union. But on the part of most of the Orange agents who carry out the hellish work, the campaign

---

* It has long been the aim of British policy to foster sectarian rancour in Ireland. Dr. Boulter, an Englishman, who was Protestant Archbishop of Armagh, from 1725 to 1738, writing of the agitation raised by Dean Swift against *Wood's Halfpence*, said : "The worst of this is that it tends to unite Protestant and Papist, and whenever that happens, good-bye to the English interest in Ireland for ever."

"That sentence epitomizes the so-called 'Ulster Difficulty'."—Professor Eoin MacNeil in the *Irish Bulletin*.

Referring to the Volunteer Movement of 1782, Thierry says : "This spirit of mutual toleration was considered by the English Government as extremely formidable ; and it employed all its policy to destroy it and to revive the old religious and national animosities."—*Hist. of Norman Conquest*, Concl. Sec. 4.

13

is simply anti-Catholic. Many of those who in North-East Ulster are popularly known as the " Unionist Leaders " would seem to be actuated by a spirit equally anti-National and anti-Catholic. In practice, however, it comes to much the same thing, as in Belfast Catholic and Nationalist are almost synonymous terms.

Inasmuch as the general public, and the Press, which must occasionally be quoted, have almost invariably used the word Catholic instead of Nationalist, it will make for clearness to do the same here.

OMENS OF PEACE.

SINCE the Pogrom of 1912, when all Catholics were temporarily driven out of the shipyard of Workman and Clark, Belfast had enjoyed a period of peace remarkable for that city. Relations between the workers of various creeds had become quite friendly.

The shipyard strike of 1919 revealed a wonderful thing in the political history of the city. There had been growing up steadily and unobtrusively a feeling of the solidarity of Labour and a tendency to forget the differences of Orange and Green in attempts to achieve objects of common interest to the workers in Belfast irrespective of creed and politics. This movement culminated in the 44-hour strike, when the shipyard workers, under the chairmanship of a Catholic trade unionist, carried the struggle almost to victory. It was probably the only occasion in the industrial history of Belfast when the reactionary employing classes of the city felt that their hold was slipping and that the old game of setting the Protestant and Catholic workers at each others' throats was failing. No observer of industrial conditions in the North could fail to be struck by the fact that sectarian bitterness was all to the interests of the employing classes and calculated to prevent the free working of the normal Trade Union activity, which is found necessary in every industrial centre if workers are to maintain anything like a decent standard of life.

WHAT A BOGUS TRADE UNION DID.

THE wire-pullers in high places were aghast at the apparent failure of the old slogans to carry disunion into the workers' camp, and after the collapse of the strike they were not long in setting to work to make sure that never again should such a situation be allowed to develop. The result was the formation of the bogus and sectarian trade union called the Unionist Labour Party, under the direction of Sir Edward Carson, and favoured by the Tory employers. The political activities of this party were completely successful in driving a solid wedge between the Protestant and Catholic workers, and in fostering among the former a spirit which was soon to show itself in the shipyard pogrom.

One can only guess at the various devices by which the Carsonist leaders stifled the growing

spirit of comradeship in the Orange working men.
But enough to know that it was done, and that
those who in January stood round the same platforms and cheered with their brother Catholics were
ready by July, at the call of Carson, to attack those
same fellow-workers with the ferocity of wild beasts.

THE FIERY CROSS.

ON the twelfth of July, 1920, at Finaghy, a suburb
of Belfast, Sir Edward Carson delivered a very
bitter speech—outlandish, one would say, for any
man holding such a responsible position—to the
assembled Orange brethren.*

Of course, it was religiously read by all his
followers in Ulster. The chief theme of the
harangue was that the loyalists of Ulster were in
imminent peril from Sinn Fein, that he was losing
hope of the Government's defending them, and that
they must be up and doing to protect themselves.
" And these are not mere words," he said ; " I
am sick of words without action."

He dragged in the Catholic Hierarchy and the
priests. The speech was altogether a good sample
of the " Raw-head-and-bloody-bones " kind and
well calculated to excite the fanatical elements.

Of course, as everyone knows, there was absolutely no menace of the kind.

* *The Times*, July 13th, in an editorial severely censuring Sir
Edward's outburst, refers to the " Twelfth " celebration the previous day as a " parade of anachronistic intolerance."

THE ORANGE PRESS TAKES UP THE CRY.

BETWEEN the 12th and the 20th, the Orange Press lent itself to the publication in a prominent way of a number of letters, some of which may be read in the Appendix. There was no camouflage regarding Sinn Fein here, but a call to battle of Protestant against Catholic in Belfast, and, we suppose, every other place where they were in a sufficient majority. The publication of such shameless letters appealing to the lowest instincts of bigotry, in staid newspapers claiming to be respectable, was surely very significant.

Another feature of the time was the continued publication day by day, for a week after the Twelfth, of speeches of extremists all over Ulster delivered on the Twelfth of July platforms urging undying conflict with the Church of Rome, and calling on the Protestants to prepare to protect themselves against an imminent danger.

COMING EVENTS.

FOR several weeks before the outburst, Catholics in the shipyards and other places had hints that trouble was brewing. Some of their less reticent Protestant mates told them as much, and even mentioned the day fixed upon—the 21st of July. They preferred, however, to treat such reports as bluster, and when " the day " arrived they went as usual to the yards.

Nearly 5000 of them were employed there, efficient men in every department of those great concerns ; 1,025 of them were ex-service men, many of whom had fought for Britain not in one but in several wars. Probably more than three-fourths of all these workers were at the time followers of Joseph Devlin, and politically opposed to Sinn Fein.

THE DAY ARRIVES—21st JULY, 1920.

A MEETING of all the Orange elements in the ship-yards was called for the dinner hour. Hundreds of chalk marks on the wall had been telling those in the know to " Remember the 21st." The meeting was a huge one, composed mainly of well-paid stay-at-homes who had had the time of their lives during the Great War, and it was addressed by men of the same stamp.

Immediately after the meeting a violent onslaught was made upon the Catholic employees as well as on a dozen or two of Protestants who refused to bow the knee to Carson. They were peremptorily ordered to clear out. Being in a minority of less than one to six, they could not put up a fight with any hope of success. Those who could get quietly away accepted the inevitable. Many came in for various kinds of attack. Hundreds were sur-rounded and kicked. Several were thrown into water, twenty-five feet deep, and pelted with bolts and other missiles as they struggled for life. Even

according to the Orange Press—which, as we shall
see, has hardly admitted any Orange delinquencies
—men swimming from their pursuers were pelted
back from the opposite bank, and one man had to
swim for safety to Sydenham, a mile distant. No
one was killed outright, but nearly a score of very
seriously injured were conveyed to hospital, and a
large number of others badly hurt were treated at
home. Since that day, now over two years ago,
no Catholic—with the exception, I understand, of
one or two office hands—has been allowed to earn
a living in Belfast's chief industrial concerns, the
shipbuilding yards. (*See letter of Councillor Baird,
a Protestant expelled, page* 30.)

LOYALISTS ALL.

WHEN all was over, and the Catholics cleared out,
a force of military arrived, and the pogromists, as
the *Northern Whig* (Protestant) informs us,
" received the forces of the law with cheers, and
the singing of loyal choruses."

OUT OF THE FRYING PAN.

THE victims of this pogrom—mostly from the district known as the Falls—went to their homes
depressed and broken enough, one may suppose.
In the evening, crowds from the notorious anti-
National district of the Shankill, not content with
what had been done, assembled at the ends of
streets leading into the Nationalist quarters and

kept up a menacing and offensive demonstration.
An ugly situation developed. The military duly
came on the scene. Some rounds were fired. Three
Nationalists, who were going about their legitimate
business, were killed and seven seriously wounded.
The Orange* aggressors got away almost without
a scratch. In the meantime, in Ballymacarrett
(which is the portion of Belfast built on the south
side of the River Lagan, and where Catholics.
number less than ten thousand out of well over a
hundred thousand), wholesale looting of Catholic
shops, and violence to Catholic residents, were
going on quite unchecked. Such are, in very brief
outline, the events of the first day of the pogrom
in Belfast.

WORKS OF THE SECOND DAY—22nd JULY, 1920.

THE second day was chiefly marked by unprecedented looting and burning of Catholic property,
especially in Ballymacarrett. (*See Map*). The
Orange mobs, many of them drunk with looted
whiskey, began early and worked late. When all
the Catholic shops in the Newtownards Road area
were cleaned out, they even looted a few belonging
to their own co-religionists. The air was thick

---

* It is not to be inferred, of course, that the mobs who attack
the persons and property of Catholics in Belfast are all enrolled
members of the Orange Order. Many of them are only aux-
iliaries. The writer throughout has preferred to use the term
" Orange " rather than " Protestant," because the former is substantially correct, and because he has been loth to associate with
such disgraceful proceedings the name of a religious body for
many of whose members he entertains the highest respect.

with burnings all day long and throughout the night. The various sections of a very efficient fire brigade were sorely overworked and much handicapped by the frequent cutting of the hose-pipes by the frenzied Protestant mobs, who in their strength defied a weak and indulgent police.

STORMING A CHURCH.

AT night a large crowd, of whom a great number were shipyard workers, attacked the Catholic Church of St. Matthew's, a handsome edifice at Bryson Street, on the Newtownards Road, and surrounded on two sides by the Orange quarters. So fierce was the assault that the military were compelled to fire, and some lives were lost.

(" *It is ridiculous to state,*" *says Sir James Craig,* "*that Catholics are being attacked on account of their religion!*)

WHAT A BRITISH OFFICER SAW.

AT the subsequent inquest, Lieutenant John F. Woodthorpe, 1st Norfolk Regiment, gave evidence. (*See Belfast Press,* 10.8.20) :

" About 7.30 p.m. on the 22nd July, witness saw a dense and hostile crowd around the Roman Catholic chapel, Bryson Street. They were climbing the railings of the chapel. Witness rushed up about eighteen men and entered the chapel grounds. They managed to clear away the crowd who were stoning the church. . . . The crowd continued stoning the chapel and the troops. Shots were fired and witness gave the order to fire."

This was one of the extremely rare instances in which the military ever fired on an Orange mob in Belfast. The jury found that "The military were justified in firing."

The same witness says in the course of his evidence :

"On the 22nd (July) dense crowds looted a number of shops on the Newtownards Road. The looting continued throughout the day. A large proportion of the crowd were in a drunken state."

FIRING ON A MONASTERY.

ON that same evening further trouble arose on the border of Shankill and Falls districts. Military fired several rounds into the Catholic quarters and upon the Redemptorist Monastery. Seven people, including one of the religious in the monastery, were shot dead by this fire, and several were wounded. The total casualties for the day were twelve dead and forty-six wounded.

The Press Association, whose correspondent in Belfast is always either an Orangeman, or in the hands of the Orangemen, gave out that "sniping took place from the tower of the monastery. This was returned by the military, who succeeded in stopping it." A deliberate falsehood, which, in spite of an official denial by the rector, was published throughout the English Press.

AND WHAT A JURY THOUGHT OF IT.

AT the subsequent inquest, a Belfast jury found that, in the case leading to Brother Morgan's death, *" the firing was entirely unnecessary for the purpose of suppressing the riot, and was unprovoked by the action of any person in the monastery."*

ORANGE BRAVES ATTACK CONVENT OF NUNS.

THE third day of the pogrom, 23.7.20, was marked by continued burnings and the eviction of large numbers of Catholics from their homes in several of the Protestant parts of the city.

At about ten o'clock at night a desperate attack was made on the convent of the Nuns of the Cross and Passion, beside St. Matthew's Church in Bally-macarrett.* The sisters, who devote their lives to teaching the children in the adjacent schools, were about to retire to rest when the convent was attacked by a furious Orange mob, supplied with petrol and weapons for breaking in the doors. Military were telephoned for, but before their arrival the furniture of two rooms had already been sprinkled with petrol and set on fire.

WHAT OFFICERS OF THE CROWN SAID ABOUT IT.

DISTRICT INSPECTOR SIDLEY, a Protestant, told at-a subsequent inquest how he went with a force of ten police and seven soldiers, and found the

* Lord Derby visited and was entertained by the nuns of this convent during his mission to Ireland in 1921.

convent being attacked by a " crowd of hundreds,"
who had got inside the railings, while thousands of
others on the Newtownards Road adjacent witnessed the attack.   That from these latter shots
were fired upon his men when trying to defend the
convent.

Constable James Carty described his journey in
a lorry through the intensely Orange district of
Newtownards Road, where the mobs were winding
up a long day's loot and burning of houses belonging to the sparse Catholic minority.

" We were assailed," he said, " by a riotous
mob on Newtownards Road.   Several fires were
ablaze in the side streets.   The crowd threw
stones, bottles, and other missiles at the lorry and
its occupants who had to shelter at the bottom of
the vehicle. At Bryson Street the rioters, number-
ing about four thousand, closed in on the vehicle,
and the military then fired three or four rounds
which had the effect of scattering the hostile forces
into side thoroughfares." Of course the crowd
were enraged at the military for going to the
defence of the burning convent.

WHAT AN ORANGE PAPER SAID ABOUT IT.

NEXT day the Orange Press took hardly any notice
of this very disgraceful incident, and the *Northern
Whig* told its readers that " the attack on the convent on Newtownards Road last night was the *work
of one or two lads.*"

A MONSTROUS, LYING PRESS.

IT may be pointed out here that the methods of the Belfast Orange Press all through the pogrom troubles would be incredible even to those familiar with the wiles of dishonest journalism in any other part of the world. A vast deal of responsibility for what has happened in Belfast during the past two years must undoubtedly be laid at the doors of three Belfast Orange newspapers and their confederates abroad. They have been very rightly described as ghouls. For suppressing the truth, and for suggesting, and evenly boldly asserting, the false, they are probably without a rival ˙ The pogrom was not sprung as a surprise on them. They knew what was coming, and they were well prepared to do their part. Sir Hamar Greenwood had just been in office for a few months. His brazen method of denying all charges made against the Black and Tans, his policy of " kill, kill, and keep shouting murderer " shocked most people, but appealed strongly to his admirers in Belfast. For instance, on the 22nd July, after the events of the previous day described at the beginning of this article, the *Belfast News Letter,* which is regarded as the most respectable of the three Orange papers, came out with its report under the following caption :

RIOTING IN BELFAST.

SERIOUS DISORDER ON FALLS ROAD.

SINN FEINERS ATTACK WORKERS.

MILITARY SHOT AT AND STONED.

THREE KILLED AND SEVERAL WOUNDED.

B

This was good for the head-line-reading multitude—such as soldiers are, for example. No reference is made there to one of the greatest events in Belfast history, in view of its results—the expulsion of all Catholics from the shipyards.

QUITE HAMARESQUE.

AND before one serious blow had been struck by the victims, and while they were being murdered and burned out of the city, the same paper writes editorially July 23rd :

" Government have a very serious situation to deal with. The Sinn Fein mobs are out armed, not for rioting in the ordinary way, but for guerilla warfare."

From this attitude these newspapers have never departed by a hair's breadth. In the midst of the wildest furies of the Orange mobs they have congratulated them and flattered them for their admirable *restraint,* " notwithstanding the *frightful provocation* " they are supposed to have received. Sir Edward Carson, and, after him, Sir James Craig, adopted the same inexcusable cant. Nothing was better calculated to assure the Orange party that there were no lengths of bloodshed and destruction against Catholics to which they might not go with impunity.

WHAT SOME OUTSIDERS HAD TO SAY.

As a sample of how unprejudiced witnesses from abroad viewed the position at this time, take from among many similar :

1.

"It is common knowledge in Belfast, and frequently admitted by individual Unionists, that plans were matured at least two months ago to drive all Home Rule workmen in the shipyards out of their employment."—Special Correspondent of the *Westminster Gazette*, 24th July, 1920.

2.

"Now that twenty people have been killed and four hundred Catholic families turned out of their homes, and £1,000,000 worth of damage done, Belfast is beginning to come to its senses. **Belfast is in its present plight and is faced with future trouble simply and solely because there has been an organised attempt to deprive Catholic men of their work, and to drive Catholic families from their homes.**"—*Daily Mail*, 1st September, 1920.

3.

"Events are developing as I anticipated. Five weeks of ruthless persecution by boycott, fire, plunder and assault, culminating in a week's wholesale violence probably unmatched outside the area of Russian or Polish pogroms, have had their inevitable result. **The Catholic Irish are arming rapidly and turning on their tormentors.** The character of the struggle is changing from hour to hour."—Hugh Martin in *Daily News*, 1st September, 1920.

ENGLISH FAIR PLAY.

HERE is an incident which must not be omitted. It shows the kind of thing which the Catholics of Belfast are too often up against.

One day early in the riots, whilst the military were protecting St. Matthew's Catholic Church, which, as we have seen above, had been violently attacked by a large Orange mob, the " loyalists " mounted two Union Jacks on the pillars of the main entrance. A day or two later the *Daily Mail* had in its news columns a large photograph reproduction of the flags, the church, and the military, under the caption :

" WHERE THE FLAG STILL FLIES "
and underneath :

" A Protestant Church (in Belfast) guarded
by his Majesty's troops against the rebels."

One of the priests of St. Matthew's wrote to the *Daily Mail* asking for a correction of the mistake, but none was ever made.

A LULL.

After an orgy of three or four days, rioting abated considerably. The reader doubtless has little desire to be told of all the minor outbreaks which occurred in the next month, during which indeed some lives were lost, several people wounded and a great deal of looting took place.

But it must be pointed out that expulsion from work was by no means confined to the shipyards. Catholic workers were expelled in large numbers from nearly all the engineering works, from most of the large factories, from warehouses, shops and concerns of every kind, until in the course of a few weeks the victims thus excluded from earning their bread totalled over 8,000. Scarcely one of them has since been allowed to return ; 1,225 of the expelled were ex-service men.

SOME WORDS OF A BISHOP.

A FUND was opened, and an appeal made to the
people of the rest of Ireland and of the world at
large on behalf of the expelled workers.   In a
letter to the Committee in charge of this fund, Most
Rev. Dr. MacRory, in forwarding a first subscrip-
tion of £100, made some apt observations which
may be quoted here :

"I am aware that it was not want of sympathy
that delayed the appeal until now. We all waited,
and I think rightly waited, to see what action
would be taken by the Trades Unions, whose
rules have been defied, and whose very existence
threatened by the authors of the Belfast outbreak.   But it now appears that, for the present,
at any rate, the Trades Unions can do very
little, and meantime the position of the expelled
workers, now nearly four weeks without work, is
becoming desperate, and their wives and children are
crying for bread.

"Every day brings me painful evidence of the
widespread and bitter destitution.   It makes one
almost despair of human nature to think that these
expelled workers have been victimised by their own
fellow-workers. Yet such is, in large measure, the
fact.   For even when all allowance is made for
secret political and capitalistc influence, and for the
unholy Carsonite incitement on the 12th of July last
to religious bigotry, the hard fact remains that it was
by fellow-workers the victims were driven from their
works and their homes wrecked and looted.

"These bullies and their sleek abettors talk glibly
of *Civil and Religious liberty*, but they appear from
their actions not to have even the most elementary
idea of what either means.

"Liberty means to them licence to do their own
sweet will.

"A few years ago they entered into a solemn
covenant binding themselves to defy not only the rest

of Ireland but George V. and the British Parliament, and now, forsooth, they won't consent to work with anyone who has not first professed his allegiance to the same George V.

"And as to Religious liberty, they have on the present occasion victimised many thousands for no other reason on earth than because they are Catholics."

AND OF A BELFAST PROTESTANT.

A LETTER from Mr. James Baird, Town Councillor, Belfast—a Protestant and expelled worker—to the Dublin *Evening Telegraph,* November 11th, 1920, and referring to the report of an incident at a meeting of Belfast Board of Guardians, may not be out of place here. He writes :

"Lest any of your readers should be misled by the report referred to, I take the liberty of putting the facts concerning Belfast before them.

"On the 21st of July, and on succeeding dates, every Roman Catholic—whether ex-service man who had proved his loyalty to England during the Great War, or Sinn Feiner who claims to be loyal to Ireland and Ireland alone—was expelled from the shipyards and other works; a number were flung into the river and while struggling for life were pelted with rivets and washers; others were brutally beaten, but the majority, hearing of the fate of their fellows, escaped injury by beating a hasty retreat, leaving behind costly tools and other personal belongings. Almost 10,000 workers are at present affected, and on several occasions men have attempted to resume work only to find the ' loyal ' men still determined to keep them out. I am informed that one Catholic has been permitted to start on the Queen's Island—one out of thousands, assuming the report is true."

AND A WORD OF PREMIER CRAIG.

AND here, too, may be recorded the disgraceful declaration made by Sir James Craig at the unfurling of a Union Jack at the shipyards on October the 14th of that same year, 1920. Referring, of course, to the pogrom, which included attacks upon a church and a small convent of nuns, he said :

"I think it only fair that I should be asked a question in return, and it is: 'Do I approve of the action you, boys, have taken in the past?' I say **'YES'.''**

He was then Parliamentary Secretary to the British Admiralty. He is now Premier of Northern Ireland. He has never retracted, but rather reiterated that shameful avowal.

THE VICTIMS.

THERE are wastrels and undesirables in every community, of course, and Catholic Belfast had not been free from them ; but nearly a hundred per cent. of the expelled workers were of the kind that would make for the credit and well-being of any city —honest, efficient, hard-working. Many of them filled well-paid positions, several of them were men of the highest expert knowledge. Mr. Davidson, head of the great Sirocco Engineering Works, in appealing to his Orange workers to try to carry on in peace with their Catholic fellow-workers, pointed out that a number of these latter were indispensables in connection with certain patents possessed by the firm.

It was extremely pathetic to see all these, through no fault of their own, but owing to the frenzied bigotry of the majority of another creed, driven out to emigrate from their own city, or face starvation, or live on the scanty alms of a charitable public.

" Yes," some will say, " but they could have got back on signing a declaration of loyalty " and repudiation of Sinn Fein. Possibly that is so.; more probably it is not. The document they were asked to sign was simply a " crawling order " so humiliating, in view of all the circumstances, that no man with any self-respect left could put his name to it. Its authors, doubtless, had this clearly in view when drawing it up.

The attitude of Lord Pirrie, head of the firm of Harland and Wolff's, was, on this occasion, quite contemptible. Shortly after the expulsions he issued an ambiguous threat about reviewing the whole situation in the course of a few days if things did not return to normal. As days and weeks passed they only became, if anything, more abnormal. Yet Lord Pirrie during the past two years has done nothing. His published threat has remained a dead letter. This one-time professing Home Ruler—whatever may have been his motives'—has stood meekly by whilst the great firm which he controls has been permanently turned into a purely Orange preserve where an Irish Nationalist or Catholic is not allowed to show his face. The mere threat of closing down the works had already on former occasions brought the Orange rowdies speedily to their senses. Why has *nothing* been done by Lord Pirrie or the other heads of the firm to restore fair play since July, 1920 ?

SECOND OUTBREAK
24th August, 1920

THE week to which the well-known *Daily News* correspondent refers above* began on the 25th of August, 1920, but the furies continued at work for nine days. The authorities had taken no advantage of the recent lull to prepare for a recrudescence which, there is good reason to believe, they foresaw almost to a certainty.

On the opening day a second attack in strong force was made by a shipyard mob on St. Matthew's Catholic Church. The place was vigorously defended, until the arrival of the military, by the local residents, assisted by a number of soldiers off duty, who, being unarmed, had to be content to use stones.

The chief features of this second outbreak were the wholesale burning of Catholic property, shops and dwellings ; looting, evictions and a very high casualty list.

* See page 27.

ONE WEEK'S BURNINGS.

THE extent of the burnings will be best understood by the official list of genuine calls to the fire brigade during that period as supplied to the Press at the time. The whole of this destruction was done by loyalist mobs. Catholics were not even accused of one act of incendiarism—then or for over a year afterwards. It has been stated, but the writer has been unable to discover any proof of it, that in a few cases houses belonging to Protestants were burned or damaged from being adjacent to houses of Catholics set on fire by the Orange mobs.

25TH AUGUST, 1920.

The calls to the Belfast Fire Brigade during the day were :—

10. 0 a.m.	Pitt St., Newtownards Road	10.45 p.m.	My Lady's Road
		10.50 ,,	Lord Street
10.30 ,,	Fox Street	11.13 ,,	Albion St., Sandy Row
7. 5 p.m.	Lawnbrook Av.		
7.47 ,,	Castlereagh Street	11.22 ,,	Templemore St.
8.19 ,,	Frome Street	11.34 ,,	Avoniel Street
8.45 ,,	Templemore Av.	11.45 ,,	Castlereagh Road
8.56 ,,	Templemore St.	11.57 ,,	Convention Street
9. 9 ,,	Corner of Erskine Street	12. 3 ,,	Isoline Street
		12.16 ,,	Isoline Street
9.41 ,,	Portobello Street	12.20 ,,	' ord Street
10. 4 ,,	Solway Street	12.37 ,,	Ravensdale Street
10. 9 ,,	Beersbridge Road	1.22 ,,	Avoniel Road
10.43 ,,	Beersbridge Road	1.22 ,,	Lord Street

26TH AUGUST, 1920.

Westbourne Street	6.55 p.m.	Seaforde Street
Hornby Street	8.21 ,,	Canton Street
Templemore St.	8.51 ,,	Beersbridge Road
Hornby Street	9.28 ,,	Albert Bridge Rd.
Dee Street	9.38 ,,	Beersbridge Road
Canton Street	10. 4 ,,	Beersbridge Road
My Lady's Road	11. 8 ,,	Newtownards Rd.
Foundry Street	11. 8 ,,	Lord Street
Belvoir Street	11.18 ,,	Templemore Av.
Westbourne Street	11 18 ,,	My Lady's Road
Solway Street	11.24 ,,	Woodstock Road
Templemore Av.	11.38 ,,	Canning Street
Templemore St.	11.44 ,,	Grove Street
Foundry Street	11.49 ,,	Castlereagh Rd.
Templemore St.	11.20 ,,	Mount Street

27TH AUGUST, 1920.

Templemore Av.	4.36 p m.	Albert Bridge Rd.
Castlereagh Road	4.49 ,,	Lawnbrook Av.
Clandeboy Street	5.17 ,,	Castlereagh Road
44 Lord Street	6.84 ,,	Castlereagh Road
My Lady's Road	7.35 ,,	Lord Street
Belvoir Street	7.35 ,,	Kenbawn Street
115 Castlereagh	8.14 ,,	Chadolly Street
Road	8.27 ,,	Castlereagh Road
Newtownards Rd.	9. 4 ,,	Foundry Street
Castlereagh Road	9.42 ,,	Chadolly Street
Charles St. south	11. 1 ,,	Eliza Street
Chadolly Street	11.47 ,,	Castlereagh Road

28TH AUGUST, 1920.

City Street	2.11 p.m.	Pernau Street
Lower Mount St.	2.11 ,,	Langley Street
Tennant Street	2.52 ,,	Carnan Street
Linfield Street	2.52 ,,	Langley Street
Hillman Street	3.54 ,,	Tennant Street
Gooseberry Street	3.56 ,,	Langley Street
Langley Street	4.15 ,,	Berlin Street
Agnes Street	6.24 ,,	Berlin Street
Byron Street	9. 0 ,,	Nixon Street
Berlin Street	9.40 ,,	Mathcett Street
Langley Street	10. 3 ,,	City Street
Tennant Street	10.20 ,,	Hillman Street
Tennant Street	10.25 ,,	Tennant Street
Silvio Street	10 45 ,,	Snugville Street
Upper Riga Street	11.41 ,,	City Street
Louisa Street	11.56 ,,	Nixon Street
Berlin Street	12. 1 a.m.	Urney Street
Oldpark Road		

29TH AND 30TH AUGUST, 1920.

11. 2 a.m.	Boundary Street		7.46 p.m.	Rosemary Street
1. 9 ,,	Gertrude Street		8. 5 ,,	Vere Street
1.20 p.m.	Sugarfield Street		8.14 ,,	Everton Street
1.25 ,,	Langley Street		8.14 ,,	Hillview Street
2.29 ,,	Wellwood Street		8.35 ,,	Glenview Street
2.50 ,,	Leadbeater Street		9. 1 ,,	Dundee Street
3.42 ,,	Snugville Street		9.15 ,.	Moscow Street
3.50 ,,	Woodvale Park		9 25 ,,	Riga Street
	Fire Alarm		9.28 ,,	Albion Street
4.45 ,,	Malvern Street		9.35 ,,	Everton Street
5. 0 ,,	Craven Street		9 37 ,,	Crimea Street
5. 5 ,,	Walton Street		9.45 ,,	Tennant Street
5.12 ,,	Conlon Street		10.18 ,,	Albion Street
6.25 ,,	Langwell Street		10 22 ,,	St. Leonard Street
6.31 ,,	Silvio Street		10.31 ,,	Rowan Street
6.31 ,,	Hemsworth Street		11.37 ,,	Bryson Street
6.36 ,,	York Street		11.28 ,,	Albion Street
7. 3 ,,	Vere Street		11.39 ,,	Agnes Street
7. 3 ,,	Dundee Street		1.12 a.m.	Agnes Street
7. 9 ,,	Agnes Street			

31ST AUGUST, 1920.

3.36 p.m.	Agnes Street		9.10 p.m.	Danube Street
3.35 ,,	Tennant Street		9.12 ,,	Hanna Street
3.54 ,,	Tennant Street		9.12 ,,	Glenfarne Street
4.23 ,,	Old Lodge Road		9.20 ,,	Rowan Street
4.24 ,,	Hanover Street		9.59 ,,	Heather Street
4.25 ,,	Unity Street		10. 0 ,,	Albion Street
4.49 ,,	St. Leonard Street		10,14 ,.	McLure Street
6.55 ,,	Brookmount St.		10.26 ,,	Florence Place
7.10 ,,	Bristol Street		10.35 ,,	Albion Street
7.53 ,,	Old Lodge Road		10.47 ,,	Bankmore Street
8.37 ,,	Agnes Street			

1ST SEPTEMBER, 1920.

3.15 a.m.	Agnes Street		1. 0 p.m.	Shankill Road
4.10 ,,	North Street		1.48 ,,	Albion Street
4.15 ,,	Library Street		1.53 ,,	Shankill Road
10 23 ,,	Dundee Street		2. 6 ,,	Agnes Street
11.20 ,,	Donegall Road		2.24 ,,	Tennant Street
11.59 ,,	St. Leonard Street		2.45 ,,	Danube Street

ANTI-CATHOLIC CAMPAIGN.

THE special correspondent of the *Daily News* writing from Belfast on the last day of August, 1920, says : —

" All but a very few of the business premises of Belfast Catholics, except those in the very heart of the city, or in the Catholic stronghold known as the Falls, have now been destroyed.

" Twenty fires were ablaze at once in the Shankill Road area last night, and the fire engines are still passing and repassing as I write.

" The total number of serious conflagrations during the past six days now stands at 180, or considerably more than one an hour over the whole of that period. If small fires were added the total would be doubled. The value of the damage is in the neighbourhood of a million sterling for the city of Belfast alone, while outlying towns have also suffered severely.

" *Practically the whole of this damage has been done to the property of Catholics.*

" But the entire body of ratepayers is legally chargeable for compensation.

" Belfast has thus been brought by the anti-Catholic campaign to the verge of bankruptcy.

" Seventeen people have been killed in street fighting, one hundred and seventy seriously injured, and at least a thousand slightly hurt.

" The quantity of goods looted from Catholics has been prodigious, and the character of the loot has naturally added to the savagery of the fighting. This sort of brigandage has been going forward to-day since early morning in the Shankill district where last night's fires occurred.

" Hundreds of workingmen's homes are now stocked with looted whiskey.

" In the old days the business of spirit grocery was one of the very few that Catholics were allowed

to carry on. Hence the trade was, up till a week
ago, very largely in their hands. It is to-day on the
point of extinction. The Catholics are, however, still
fighting with the fury of desperation. Although it is
impossible to save their shops, they are making a
stand for their homes."

VÆ VICTIS.

DURING the first day of this outbreak Ballymacarrett was the chief storm centre. In addition
to a second attack on St. Matthew's Church, the
Orange shipyard workers made an onslaught on
a number of defenceless Catholics working at the
coal quays which has not been surpassed for
savagery since the trouble began. The usual
surging crowds came along from the yards, and,
finding some of their old Catholic "mates" who
had been expelled, and had taken work unloading
coal at the quays, they fell upon them with every
available weapon of attack   Some of them were
beaten with sticks and kicked to unconsciousness ;
others were hurled into the water or coal bunkers ;
a few escaped in shirt and trousers   A more disgraceful or more cruel performance could not well
be imagined.

ATTEMPT TO BURN A CHILD.

ON the same day, 26th August, during a general
riot and the burning of thirty-six houses of Catholics
in Ballymacarrett, the house of a Mrs. McLean
was burned. Her little girl of six was knocked
down and actually kicked by a full-grown member

of the Orange crowd. A bottle of petrol was poured on the child and an attempt made to set her on fire. The mother managed to drag her away, and fought her way out of the crowd into a Catholic quarter.

KEEPING THE RING!

AN undertaker's shop and the shop of a man called Lennon were burned on the Newtownards Road with the military " on duty " standing inactive a few yards away.

The Orange rowdies were allowed to march in thousands behind armoured cars, under the very shelter of which they repeatedly fired into Catholic streets, especially Seaforde Street.

"I saw," says the special correspondent of the *Daily Mail*, "huge heaps of paving stones, the favourite ammunition of the Belfast street-fighter. The Orangemen invariably fight under the Union Jack, and, when the soldiers appear, the rioters wave the flag and shout, ' We are loyalists'."

EVICTIONS.

DURING this frightful time Catholic families in hundreds were evicted from their homes by the Orange party in most of the Protestant quarters. At least a couple of thousand people were driven out in this way. Large numbers of them were given a shelter in the already congested Nationalist areas, hundreds had to lodge in schoolhouses, stores and even stables. Several slept in tents on ground adjoining churches. Large numbers of still more unlucky ones had to wander the streets in fruitless search all day, and sleep in the open by night. Of course, their eviction left far more houses in the hands of the loyalist mobs than they could get people of their own to occupy. A few Protestants from Catholic districts made friendly exchanges with Catholics in Protestant quarters. Many others when asked to do so refused. In a relatively small number of cases—not over sixty at most—Protestants were compelled to clear out Eviction of this kind did not leave them homeless, as they could find ample accommodation in houses from which Catholics had been driven.

It may have been a coincidence, but at any rate it is a fact, that the "competent military authority" which had looked on without a word or a gesture whilst hundreds of Catholic families were being ruthlessly thrown out became suddenly active and vocal as soon as a few Protestants were interfered with. General Bainbridge, head of the Forces in Belfast, issued a strong order against the evictions, declaring that "this barbarism must cease." As a matter of fact it has never ceased on the part of the Orange mobs.

CURFEW.

CURFEW was imposed on the city on the 30th of August, and had the immediate effect of easing the situation so far as street fighting was concerned.

The remainder of the year had no further outbursts so violent as those of July and August, but was not without frequent troubles and some ghastly tragedies.

One of these latter occurred on the night of the 26th of September, and marks the first appearance in Belfast of undisguised murder by forces of the Crown. A policeman had been shot dead and another wounded at a place called Broadway at about eleven o'clock at night. After midnight, three most respectable men were dragged from their beds and murdered in cold blood by members of the R.I.C. There is no doubt whatever as to what the murderers were; in fact they seemed to take little or no pains to hide their identity. The names of the victims were Edward Trodden, John McFadden and James Gaynor.

AN ATTACK ON A CHURCH.

A SERIOUS occurrence took place in what is known as the Marrowbone district, a small Catholic colony of little over a thousand in the midst of a surrounding Protestant population of at least forty to one. This unfortunate locality had been fearfully harried by the Orange rioters ever since July. For the second time within a few weeks, the Catholic Church of the Sacred Heart there was, on the 16th October, fired at with revolvers and stones by a large Orange crowd returning from a football match in the vicinity.

FLEEING WITH A CORPSE.

SOME of the shots passed through the windows of a house belonging to a Mrs. O'Neill which was in the line of fire. She was waking her dead child at the time. In the middle of the tumult she took up the corpse from the bed and fled with it by a back way and through the streets to a place of greater safety. A number of Catholic youths assisted the police in trying to hold back the assailants. The military arrived in an armoured car, ran over and killed one man on the street, fired and killed a couple more, and wounded several. The Orange crowd ran off helter-skelter, seeking shelter even in a number of Catholic houses. In no case were they refused admission.

WHAT ANANIAS SAID.

THE Orange Press, as usual, wrote up reports next day of how harmless Protestants, innocently returning from a football match, were, suddenly and without any provocation, fired upon by murderous Sinn Fein gunmen from the side streets. There is no suggestion whatever that the Protestants began the trouble by attacking the Catholic church.

WHAT A JURY SAID.

FOUR Catholic young men, arrested on this occasion for using firearms, were tried at the following Winter Assizes, December 11th, 1920, and found guilty. The Jury—chiefly non-Catholic—added a rider :

" We recommend the prisoners to the greatest mercy of the judge because of the extreme provocation they received owing to the attack on their place of worship."

His Lordship remarked that that was a very wise and discriminating verdict.

A JUDGE'S REMARKS.

AT the Winter Assizes held in Belfast a large number of loyalists were charged on remand with various outrages, mostly of a very serious kind, perpetrated upon Catholics during the course of the riots. Mr. Justice Pim, at the opening of the proceedings said, as reported in the Press :

" It was a terrible thing, because one section differed from another, that men belonging to the smaller section, no matter what the provocation, should be driven out of their work, that their wives and children should be attacked and their houses burned. That was a shocking state of affairs, and one which he knew well—because he had lived in Belfast—that the great mass of Belfast citizens were heartily ashamed of and very indignant about."

Of course the blessed word " provocation " was to be expected in the circumstances. It may also be remarked that the " majority " of Belfast citizens have managed most effectually to conceal their feelings of " shame and indignation " now for two full years.

GRIEVED BY BELFAST PERJURY.

THE same Mr. Justice Pim also said, on January
the 19th, 1921' that he was glad it was the last
day of the Assizes, for he had been greatly grieved
by the amount of perjury which he had heard all
through the proceedings.   Undoubtedly, he said,
there had been a riot on the occasion of the last
case, and it would have been sufficient for the witnesses (Orange) for the defence to have said
that the accused were not there ; but they said that
there had been *no riot at all.*

WANTED A VICTIM.

THE trial of Henry McGrath, a Catholic youth, on
the capital charge for the fatal shooting of Joseph
McLeod, a Protestant, affords a fair example of
how far the Orange party will go in their determination to secure a victim from the Catholic side.   A
long array of witnesses for the prosecution swore,
one after another, that they were present and
plainly saw McGrath, whom they had known well
for years, fire the shot which killed McLeod, that
thereupon he waved his cap and cried " Up the
Rebels," with several other details.   The evidence
of an expert witness for the defence submitted that
it would have been impossible for McGrath to have
shot McLeod from the place where those people
swore he was stationed at the time, and the jury
were requested to go and examine for themselves.
The trial was adjourned and the jury (mainly

Protestants) did so, and were quite satisfied. McGrath was declared " Not guilty." As a matter of fact it would appear that this young man had never handled any firearm in his life. The whole evidence in the case, as given in the Press, is well worth reading. There can be no question but that there was a conspiracy to swear away the life of an innocent person and wholesale perjury. Yet none of the witnesses were proceeded against on that count.

At the end of the same Assizes the *Irish News,* the local Nationalist paper, had good reason to write :

" Active instruments of the pogrom have for the most part no reason for complaint. Many of them were cheerfully acquitted—against the weight of the evidence; others were reluctantly convicted; in a large majority of cases the sentences passed were quite incommensurate with the crimes clearly proved. It is to be feared that several members of the community will regard rioting, incendiarism, looting, and other forms of plundering as forms of amusement, combining pleasure and profit with a minimum of peril, after the experience of the last seven weeks in the law courts. However, it is well that even a modicum of justice was done in some cases."

WHAT THE MINORITY ARE UP AGAINST.

THE PRESS.

THE story of Belfast during the period already under review is one of aggression and persecution

of an eminently ferocious kind by the Orange
majority against the Catholic minority. Of course
nobody expects that the persecutors will admit
this, though the whole facts of the case cry out in
condemnation against them. They have immense
advantages on their side in trying to cloak their
guilt or even to transfer it to their victims. The Press
is their great weapon ; for no judicial inquiries have
been held, and the Belfast Government have clearly
made up their minds that none shall be held. And
see how the Press stands. The Orange party have
three strong daily papers, with a wide local and
considerable overseas circulation. Financial con-
siderations alone keep them from amalgamation, for
they all cry with the same political and sectarian
voice.

NEWS AGENCIES.

IN the offices of one or other of these three Orange
papers are found, as has been said, the correspondents of all the principal news agencies and of
many of the great journals abroad. They have
confederates in England, Scotland, America and
elsewhere who chant the daily chorus with them.
When anything important takes place in Belfast
their version of it is round the world without a
moment's delay. Where Catholics are concerned
such reports are hardly ever fair, are often partly
false, and sometimes entirely so. When a lie gets
a good start the truth has little chance of overtaking
it.

The Catholics of Belfast have been cruelly handi-capped in this matter of Press propaganda. They possess only one daily newspaper, a bright and well-written one, but its local circulation is small, and its influence outside practically nil. The Ulster Protestant counts chiefly on British public opinion, and he has the bulk of the British Press ready to mould that opinion in his favour. The Ulster Catholic has few journalistic friends across the Channel, and hardly a paper to publish a half-column in his favour without a grudge.

CATCH-CRIES.

THE Orangeman seems to live and to thrive on catch-cries. But the catch-cries upon which he has relied most during all the atrocities he has been committing on his Catholic neighbours are these two : " Sinn Fein Gunmen " and " Provocation."

When the Orangemen from day to day made the Catholic quarters, such as Ballymacarrett, a hell ; when their snipers manned the house-tops and even when they carried their rifles openly in the streets under the eye of the Crown forces, the Orange Press had but one cry—" Outrages of Sinn Fein Gunmen." It did not matter that a number of Catholics were killed, and nobody killed but Catholics—the cry still went up : " The Sinn Fein Gunmen." And, of course, the cry has largely prevailed ; their friends in Britain believe—partly because they wish so to believe—that most of the crimes in Belfast are due to " Sinn Fein Gun-men."

Their other great cry is " Provocation." When they started out on the pogrom, drove the Catholics out of work, and were trying to burn them out of the whole city, their papers told them to continue to practise their well-known restraint, notwith-standing the *" frightful provocation "* which was being offered them.   Carson himself sent a message in the same terms from London when they were in a very frenzy of crime against a helpless minority.

THE ODDS.

RIOTING, or sectarian trouble of any kind, has always had a special horror for the Belfast Catholic. He knows from long experience the overwhelming forces arrayed against him.   He is like a man in his shirt against three armed men in an armoured car.

The Unionist party are more than three to one against him numerically.   They control every department of the civic administration.   The heads of the police are of their very own ; the heads of the military are the guests in their drawing-rooms, the habitues of their clubs, often of the private " lodges."   Their law courts, at least in times of turmoil, are redolent as a rule of strong partisanship.   He is liable to suffer at the hands of employers, to be attacked by fellow-workers. If a row gets up on the street the batons of the police—even those of his own co-religionists—and the rifles of the military are in nine cases out of ten turned on him. He has seen too often the aggressive Orange mobs assisted by the forces of the Crown, shielded and encouraged by the agents of the law. He has no stomach for a fight under such conditions.

THE ORANGE VERSION.

WHEN the Orange party, acting promptly on the summons to carry out an anti-Catholic pogrom, had already shocked the feelings of many people in these islands and beyond, and found themselves challenged by British Trade Unionism, they thought it well to advance some kind of excuse for their inhuman actions.

Several rather conflicting ones were put forward by their apologists. One was that the whole onslaught was a reprisal for the death of a Banbridge man killed in Cork! Sufficient evidence, however, went to show clearly that the campaign was already planned in detail weeks, at least, before anything happened to the Banbridge man. Sometimes they said it was a rising up against Sinn Fein violence in Belfast, more frequently that it was on account of Sinn Fein outrages in other parts of Ireland.

The story that came to hold the field, and which

their spokesmen have on the points of their tongues,
is as follows :

When the call went out for men to defend the
Empire in the Great War the Protestants of the
shipyards rushed to the colours in great numbers,
leaving well-paid jobs vacant behind. These were
soon taken by Sinn Fein shirkers from the " South
and West." When the War was over and won,
the men from the shipyards, who were promised
that their jobs would be kept for them on their
return, came back to find that those jobs were now
filled by shirkers, and that they themselves were
compelled to walk the streets idle. After a while,
they say, human nature asserted itself. The intruders were driven out, and the returned warriors
reinstated.

This is an attractive story, no doubt. Let us
examine the facts a little.

(a) It is doubtful if even as many as 5 per cent.
of the shipyard workers ever went out of the
country or fired a shot in the War. For reasons
probably best known to Carson and his *entourage*
the vast majority of those who did " join up " were
speedily brought back and re-employed in the shipyards and engineering concerns as " munition
workers " at bloated wages. Their jobs were
never in question. In proportion to their number,
at least as many Catholic as Protestant shipyard
workers went out and fought.

(b) At no time during the War were there more

than a handful of people from the South and West
working in the Belfast shipyards, and most of those
were sent at the request of the heads of those firms
from branches of the Labour Exchange.

(c) Over 90 per cent. of those driven from work
—chiefly by stay-at-homes—were citizens of Belfast. Over two thousand women and girls were
expelled and are still excluded from employment in
factories, warehouses, etc. What is the reason in
their case ?

(d) Catholics of North and South had done at
least as much as their Protestant fellow-countrymen
to help to win the War—all cant and blowing of
horns notwithstanding. It may not be remembered
that some thousands of Catholics were drafted into
the " Ulster " Division in an effort to bring it up
to strength.

(e) Fully 20 per cent. of the Catholics expelled
from the shipyards were ex-soldiers.

LET THE TRUTH BE KNOWN EVERYWHERE.

No persecuted people, perhaps, have ever had such
a cause to put before the world. Yet such is the
power of strong, unscrupulous Press propaganda,
that to-day two out of every three people in England and elsewhere think that Belfast " loyalists "
are being frightfully treated, and even murdered,
by Catholics called Sinn Feiners ; and a few months
ago the Orange Premier, Sir James Craig, said he
was dead against introducing martial law lest people

in England might think one side was as bad as the other ! *The Turk has the Armenian in the dock charged with massacre, and is seemingly on the point of securing a conviction.*

THE ORANGE SPECIAL POLICE.

EVEN before the actual outbreak of the pogrom the leaders of Ulster Orangeism showed clearly that they were determined to have Orangeism armed, and that, too, by the British Government. This was clear from Sir Edward Carson's speech on the Twelfth of July, and from the speeches on nearly every platform in Ulster that day.

The Ulster Volunteer Force—which in this connection is only another name for the rabble of the Orange lodges—were to be reorganised and armed, of course.

" THE TIMES " DISAPPROVES.

NEXT day (13th July, 1920) the London *Times* said editorially :

" If, indeed, that organisation were revived as a defensive police force for Ulster the most serious consequence would almost certainly ensue. Upon Sir Edward Carson lies largely the blame for having sown the dragon's teeth in Ireland. We cannot but warn him that, whatever provocation Sinn Fein may have offered to Ulster Unionism, the British people are not prepared to endorse any counter-provocation from the Ulster Volunteers."

The Government turned down Carson's proposal and the Ulster Press and the Ulster lodges showed much wrath.

THE GOVERNMENT SURRENDERS TO CARSON.

THEN the pogromists broke loose on their fiendish work in Belfast. Carson's proposal, so shocking even in the best of times to those who know the North-east, ought now to have seemed, not only grotesque, but unthinkable. But the agitation was kept up in the Press and all kinds of underhand influences were at work. Will it be believed that the pogromists of the shipyards had the audacity to send a deputation to the Government in London demanding to be organised into a police force and armed? Will it be believed, too, that the Government showed signs of surrender immediately after, and sent over Sir James Craig, who was then Secretary to the Admiralty, as their representative to discuss the subject with the Ulster Unionist Council?

To the Catholics of Belfast the whole scheme was too revolting for serious thought or question. The Press outside Belfast and one or two papers across the water were very outspoken. ·

" THE TIMES " AND " DAILY MAIL."

THE special correspondent of *The Times* wired his paper from Belfast (1st September) :

"I understand that the private meeting of the Ulster Unionist Council to be held on Friday will be addressed by Sir James Craig on behalf of the Government. The purpose of the meeting will be to discuss an offer which has been made to the Government that the Ulster Volunteers should be taken over by the military authorities and used as a force for maintain-

ing order in the province of Ulster. The suggestion
is that the Government should arm and equip them.
.   .   .   . Moderate men with whom I discussed the
matter to-day said they could hardly believe that the
Government would take such a dangerous step as to
arm the Ulster Volunteers and use them anywhere in
Ireland. Such action, in their view, would produce
most disastrous results. . . . . *Open civil war
could hardly be avoided.*"

The *Daily Mail* said (15th September, 1920) :

" It is not very surprising that the official proposal
to arm 'well disposed' citizens to 'assist the
authorities' in Belfast should have raised serious
question of the sanity of the Government. It seems
to me to be the most outrageous thing which they
have ever done in Ireland. . . . . A citizen of
Belfast who is ' well disposed ' to the British Government is almost, from the nature of the case, an
Orangeman, or, at any rate, a vehement anti-Sinn
Feiner. *These are the very people who have been
looting Catholic shops and driving thousands of Catholic
women and children from their homes.*
" We hope it may still be possible to stay the
horrors which the execution of this incredible order
will almost certainly entail. If it is not, and if the
expected results follow, there can be no hope left of
rehabilitating the shaken credit of the British Government in Ireland."

SINNING AGAINST THE LIGHT.

THE British Government, in the face of all protest,
proceeded to organise and arm those Orange hordes
—pogromists, looters, incendiaries and untried
murderers a goodly portion of them—under the
name of a Special Police Force. It need only be
said here, as their records up to date clearly show,
that, *as a body,* their misdeeds surpass the worst

that was ever anticipated. It would be unfair, in making this statement, not to add that there are, no doubt, many respectable and well-meaning men to be found amongst them.

THE BOYCOTT.

THE ruthless expulsion of thousands of Nationalists from their employment in Belfast and some other industrial centres in the North-East, the killing and wounding of many of them, the wholesale burning of their shops and dwellings, the systematic looting, wrecking and eviction naturally aroused the fiercest indignation in other parts of Ireland. When it was seen that not one protesting voice was raised from the Protestant side, the National resentment turned against Unionist Belfast as a whole. Belfast has been the shopkeeper for the greater part of the country. That Belfast men were satisfactory in commercial dealings no one was going to deny. But they seemed to think themselves indispensable and that was what nobody was going to admit.

A number of Protestant merchants in the South, who had long been traders with the Ulster capital, ashamed of the conduct of their co-religionists there, decided to break all business connections with Belfast until people there began to behave in a less barbarous manner. This movement spread, and in August an appeal was made to Dáil Eireann, as the National authority, to impose a ban on Belfast trade with the rest of Ireland. The

Dáil did not act precipitately. It issued a decree declaring it illegal to impose a religious or political test as a condition of employment in industrial concerns. In Belfast such tests continued to be imposed in defiance of this decree. An embargo was in due course placed upon Belfast trade.

Opinions differ as to the wisdom of such a course and a good deal has been said and written *pro* and *con.* Into that question it is not necessary to enter further here. Enough to say that the wholesale merchants of Belfast and four other northern towns, specially named, suffered very severely, that many industries catering largely for Irish trade were sorely crippled, that northern banks with branches throughout the country were badly hit, and that indirectly a great many other interests were affected.

The boycott, no doubt, was well deserved, but it was a drastic and unpleasant measure ; and all Irishmen, North and South, sincerely hope that present troubles may end in some reasonable settlement which will remove for ever the causes that led to such action being taken.

SECOND YEAR, 1921

A SUMMARY

THE first three months of 1921 were relatively quiet in Belfast. During that time only twelve lives were lost through violence, and probably not more than twice that number seriously wounded. Holding-up and highway robbery were now becoming things of daily occurrence in Belfast and surroundings.

MURDER BY CROWN FORCES.

ON the evening of April 23rd, two members of the Auxiliary Police were fired at and shot in Donegall Place. During Curfew the following night Patrick and Daniel Duffin, two of the most respected and well-conducted Catholic young men in the city, were very brutally murdered in their homes by members of the local R.I.C. Their funeral was made a public demonstration of respect and protest.

As a sample of lying propaganda, it may be recorded that a certain News Agency sent out photographs, which were widely published in America under the description :

> " In strife-stricken Belfast—Scene at funeral of the brothers Patrick and Daniel Duffin, members of the Auxiliary Force of the R.I.C., murdered by Sinn Feiners."

As a matter of fact their coffins were wrapped in the Republican colours and carried behind the hearse by relays of the I.R.A.

Here is a summary of the chief events of the remaining months of 1921 :

MAY.

3.—Appointment of Catholic Viceroy strongly resented by "loyalist" speakers, especially Councillor Twaddell.

7.—District Inspector Ferris attacked and seriously wounded in Cavendish Street.

18.—"Loyalists" behave very badly in various areas. A procession with band on Newtownards Road fired heavily into Catholic streets, killing one man, John Smyth, and wounding several.

22.—*Election Farce.*—Polling day. Election rendered a complete farce in all loyalist parts of the city by Orange savagery and intimidation. Revolvers, knives, sticks, stones, assaults on personation agents, smashing of vehicles, etc. used to prevent Nationalists from recording their votes. Nineteen serious hospital cases. Authorities took no serious steps to protect the minority. No counter-charge made against Nationalist in Nationalist districts.

25.—Further disturbances. Thomas Reilly, R.C., Butler Street, shot dead.

Statistics for May: Six people—all Catholics—killed.
Forty-two people—mostly Catholics—wounded.

JUNE.

10.—Constable Glover killed, and Constables Sullivan and Sharkey wounded.

10.—*First Bomb.*—Squabble in York Street area develops into serious rioting. Large Orange mob invades Dock Street. Bomb thrown into Catholic quarter, Dock Lane, seriously wounds three persons, one of whom succumbs later. Twenty hospital cases.

12.—*Dark Murder.*—In the early hours of this morning, and during Curfew, three shocking murders were perpetrated, clearly by one or other branch of the Crown Forces. The victims, who were taken from their beds, brought off some distance in motors, shot dead and then left lying by the wayside, were: Alexander McBride (30), publican; Malachy Halfpenny (22), ex-soldier; William Kerr (26), hairdresser. All three were Catholics.

12.—Three additional Catholics and one Protestant killed in York Street area. Five wounded. The two Catholics, Patrick Milligan and Joe Millar, were murdered in their own homes by men in uniform.

13.—Sniping prevalent. Orange gunmen fire on police protecting Catholic workers outside Gallagher's tobacco factory in Protestant area.   Several houses wrecked and people injured.   The house of Mrs. Kerr, 42, Vere Street, was attacked and partly wrecked.   She had received a **letter from the King** only that morning with memorial placque for her husband who had died in the War.   She is a Catholic.

14.—Centre of the Catholic district of Falls Road in a state of siege throughout a great part of the day. Houses looted.   Three killed and seven wounded.

15.—More sniping.   Catholic policeman and Catholic barman wounded.

15.—Funerals of five Catholic victims to-day. Shocking details revealed of the murders of Milligan and Millar by *men in uniform who are said to have been Special Constables.*

Mrs. Milligan says of death of her husband, John Milligan (24) on the 12th, that he was *murdered by Specials* with bayonets on rifles.

They pulled John out of a shed in the yard, saying, " Come out—you bastard, you," and shot him dead at 10 p.m., Sunday, 12th June.   They then threw the wife and child out on the street.

Four Specials burst open the door of Joseph Millar, 2, Dock Lane, when he was preparing for bed. They did not speak, but pulled Millar downstairs. He asked to get speaking to his wife and child.   They replied by obscene expressions.   They dragged him to the street and shot him dead there.

20.—It has been ascertained that the number of Catholic families evicted during the past few days amounts to close on 150.   One of them was Patrick O'Hare, his wife and children, of Urney Street. O'Hare was a **soldier of the Connaught Rangers,** home on furlough and in uniform.   The ' loyalists ' dragged him out of his home and threatened to shoot him if he did not clear out of the locality.

Statistics for June: Fourteen killed;   seventy-six wounded.

JULY.

7.—Shooting.   Raids.   Fierce attack on Catholic seamen on steamship " Baltic " by Orange mob. Men beaten and driven off the ship.

9.—Midnight. Beginning of an unprecedented display of frightfulness. Lorries of Crown Forces invade Raglan Street in the heart of the Catholic district. Mindful of recent Saturday night murders by uniformed men, a number of residents go out into the street and attack the invading force, whom they drive off for the time, with one dead and two wounded and an armoured lorry out of action.

10.—*Bloody Sunday*.—Unparalleled display by Orange mobs, assisted by Special Police and other Crown Forces; 123 houses burned, according to Dublin Castle report. Number actually burned, 161. All these were houses of Catholics. No houses of Protestants burned. Fifteen people killed, 68 serious hospital cases. Large numbers of wounded treated at home.

This outburst was evidently intended to make difficult or impossible the observance of the Truce, between Ireland and England already signed and coming into operation on July 11.

Referring to the burnings of 161 Catholic houses, the *News Letter* of July 11 characteristically says, " Fires *broke out* at a number of dwelling-houses and much damage was done by the flames." Not a hint that Orange mobs publicly burned them all !

11.—Authorities decide upon removing armed Specials of Class B. from the streets altogether, and disarming the A. Class, who wear uniform and are paid like policemen.

Note.—The order was never seriously carried out, as many subsequent events show.

12.—Sir James Craig, called to task on the Orange platform by the extremist, Sam McGuffin, surrenders and declares, "I prefer to lead the Sam McGuffins of the crowd rather than those who are apathetic, etc."

13.—Military openly defied during Curfew in some of the Orange districts of Ballymacarrett.

14.—Catholic houses wrecked in Ballymacarrett. Attacks with revolvers, etc. Two Catholics killed. Twenty-eight hospital cases.

Among the seriously wounded on this date was District Inspector McConnell. He is a Catholic, and was shot by Unionists, who cheered when they saw him fall. He had given evidence against two of their number in court at the beginning of the year. A sergeant accompanying him was shot in the wrist at the same time. Mr. Grant, Unionist M.P., who is said by eye-witnesses to have been leading the mob, was wounded.

14.—House of Miss Mary Leonard, a Catholic, *bombed* in Garmoyle Street.

15.—One, a Catholic, killed. Twenty-eight wounded. General Orange shooting continues, and, of course, the Orange Press—*notwithstanding that nearly all the victims are Catholics*—continues to cry "Sinn Fein Gunmen," and to tell the murderous Orange crowds to continue their well-known good behaviour in spite of "fearful provocation" they are receiving from Catholics. The sniping into Catholic areas in several parts of the city has been very intense for several days past, and even the arrival of large forces of police and military has little permanent effect.

15.—Shops and dwelling-houses of Catholics, especially in Ballymacarrett, wrecked and looted, and seven burned.

Two dead (Catholics) and four wounded.

21.—Children of Milltown (Catholic) Industrial School attacked and stoned by gang of men from Sandy Row.

22.—American White Cross delegation in Belfast. Visited ruins of 161 Catholic houses wrecked or burned in a single day (Sunday, July 10) by Orange mobs protected by Special Police. Mr. France—head of the delegation representing the American Committee for Relief in Ireland—" As an American citizen, I cannot comprehend how such a thing could occur in a law-abiding community. . . . .

" It is a very terrible thing to contemplate that people should be burned out of their homes and left without anything but the clothes on their backs."

One thousand homeless people huddled together in schools, old stores, stables, etc. All these are Catholics. No Protestants homeless.

Statistics for July: Twenty-six killed; 140 wounded; 216 houses (of Catholics) burned.

AUGUST.

5.—Three cases of robbery under arms.

7.—Eoin O'Duffy, T.D., Liaison Officer, says: "Entire Nationalist population of Belfast are loyally observing the Truce and, despite provocation, they still maintain the utmost forbearance."

8.—City Coroner compliments Father Murray, Adm. of St. Mary's, on his great bravery in assisting in having William McCartney, a Protestant, removed to hospital. There was much shooting at the time. Deceased was crawling on the ground fatally wounded. It was a very dangerous situation.

13.—Violent attack by about thirty Orangemen armed with revolvers on Catholic workers discharging coal boat. One shot in head and lung, another in the arm. The rest escaped.

15.—Sir James Craig invited to London Conference.

18.—At inquest on a child of thirteen, Mary McGowan, a Catholic, shot in Derby Street, the jury, after an hour's consultation, found " that Mary

McGowan died on the 21st ultimo at the Mater Hospital of a gunshot wound in the thigh, the result of being fired at by Special Constabulary, and we think that in the interests of peace the Special Constabulary should not be allowed into any locality occupied by people of an opposite denomination.''

21.—*A serious bomb outrage.*—A high explosive bomb hurled from Hanover Street (Protestant) into Tyrone Street (Catholic). Six seriously wounded. Only two Protestant families in Tyrone Street. One of these got warning before the bomb was thrown. A little boy from the other was on the street and among the wounded.

21.—A fight occurred between gunmen of both parties in the North Queen Street area. A bomb was thrown into the Catholic quarter but did not explode.

27.—*And another.*—High explosive bomb thrown into the house of Peter Moan, a Catholic, in Nelson Street. Moan is an ex-soldier from the Dorset Regiment and a well-known boxer. The family consists of ten, and the intention was evidently to make a holocaust. The house was wrecked, but, by good luck, most of the inmates were out of the way and no one was killed. This is the third bomb outrage in a week.

27.—During Curfew hours to-night in Manor Street a strange shooting affair took place between two '' B.'' Specials, who are supposed to be withdrawn, and a detective constable of the R.I.C. Two of the Specials wounded. The detective's name is Pogue. They attempted to shoot him, but he was too quick for them.

27.—*Coote calls for More Aggressiveness.*—At an Orange meeting of the Grand Black Preceptory at Newtownards, on the 12th August, Mr. William Coote, Member of the Northern Parliament, Orange Leader and '' friend '' of the Premier, urged his hearers to be '' more aggressive '' in their methods.

29.—*And the Tools Obey*—Anniversary of bloody riot. Two killed and several wounded. Bomb thrown into Catholic end of Vere Street fails to explode.

30.—*A Terrible Day.*—Five killed and twenty-eight serious hospital cases. Dozens of others treated but not detained. Christian Brother assaulted and chased in Donegall Street. Catholics had been warned for some days previously by Protestant friends that a big drive was intended.

Military withheld, and town chiefly in the hands of Special Police and R.I.C.

Besieged.—Correspondent of *Daily News* writes to his paper:

" "The practically beleaguered Catholics of the North Queen Street area, which has been in a state of siege since Monday, are asking tragically, 'Who is in control of Belfast?' The Victoria Military Barracks is right in the midst of the fighting zone, yet, with the exception of armoured car crews, not a soldier has been sent out. On the last occasion of rioting in this district, when the military were placed at street corners, the **trouble ended instantly.** Is it at all strange that the attack on the district is regarded as part of a Unionist plot to show the people of England and Scotland that no settlement is possible in Ulster?"

N.B.—Of course the Truce negotiations were at this time proceeding in London.

31.—The Orange Press continues, as usual, to cry out " Sinn Fein Gunmen."

Organised bands of " loyalists " active in all parts of the city to-day. Eight dead and sixty detained in hospital. Many lesser casualties.

Orange forces seem to be free to act as they please in all mixed portions of the city.

Statistics for August: Twenty-three dead; 165 wounded.

SEPTEMBER.

1.—Military pickets everywhere. Gunmen generally keep indoors. Catholic girls working in tobacco factory in York Street attacked fired upon from Grove Street, and compelled to turn home. Military called out. Comparative quiet restored.

2.—Occasional shooting and wounding.

2.—House of Charles Doherty, a Catholic, 36, Boundary Street, *bombed.* Terrific explosion, house wrecked and Mrs. King (daughter) seriously injured.

6.—The special correspondent of the *Manchester Guardian*, writing to his paper on the latest outbreak, says (*inter alia.*):

"After a disinterested investigation, the conclusion one has been forced to is, that the blame for **beginning the trouble** lies at the door of the Orangemen, and that for the desperate shooting of Monday and Tuesday **both sides** must bear responsibility, with this point to be remembered in favour of the Catholics, that as they were attacked, and as there was no military protection available, the members of the I.R.A. retaliated in kind and quite as effectively. Then came the call for the military.

"A week ago Mr. William Coote, M.P., was telling his friends, several thousands of them belonging to the Black Preceptory, that they must be 'more aggressive.' If the people who had achieved the expulsion of fully 3000 [5000] workers from the ship-yards were failing of aggressiveness, then the Catholic inhabitants of North Queen Street and Falls Road had some grounds for uneasiness about the next step."

After relating bomb and other outrages on Catholics, the correspondent proceeds:

"I have it on evidence that I cannot doubt, that the week's disorders began by Unionists from the

York Street area sniping into Catholic areas about
North Queen Street on Monday. This is the region
where most of the fighting occurred."

18.—Loyalists renew " aggressiveness " despite
presence of Crown forces. Violent scenes in York
Street area. Rifles, revolvers and hand grenades
used. Several wounded. Military fire on the Orange
mob in Vere Street. Result: two Protestant girls
fatally shot. Some others wounded. Orange in-
vasion of Seaforde Street area successfully repelled
by residents until military and police arrive.

23.—*Ex-Service Men Fiercely Assailed.*—One
of the most disgraceful attacks since the beginning
of the trouble was made by the Orange mobs of
Ballymacarrett to-day on some thirty Catholic ex-
service men employed in relaying the tram lines on
the Newtownards Road. The district is entirely
Protestant, and the mob is said to have been at
least two thousand strong. Of the hundred ex-
service men employed on this section, under a
London contracting firm, one-third were Catholics.
They were assailed and beaten in such a brutal
manner as could be witnessed only in Belfast.
Several of them were removed to hospital. No
one who could be identified as a Catholic escaped
unhurt.

Some of the Protestant witnesses of the outrage
expressed their unqualified horror and shame, but
were powerless to prevent it.

In the whole of the Ballymacarrett area this day
the sparse Catholic population were subjected to
very violent attacks. Many people were injured
and one killed. Orange gunmen raided at will and

actually penetrated into Catholic streets, carrying
brand new rifles and Webley revolvers.

24.—The sickening carnage goes on. Five
have been killed and over fifty seriously wounded
to-day. One of these, Murtagh McAstocker, a
Catholic youth of twenty-three, was recognised on
coming out of St. Matthew's Church, where he had
just been to confession, when he was deliberately
shot dead in the street by one of a gang of
"loyalists." When the ambulance came to pick up
the body of the youth, it was surrounded by an
Orange crowd who gave an incredible display of
savagery. See Press reports.

25.—Bombs exchanged in Ballymacarrett. One
thrown into a dense Orange crowd attacking the
Seaforde Street area had disastrous results, two men
being killed on the spot and thirty-four admitted to
hospital badly injured. It is stated that this was
an unexploded bomb promptly returned upon the
crowd from which it was first thrown.

Children bombed.—A bomb was thrown from an
Orange gang into a group of Catholic children playing in Milewater Street,* off York Road.

26.—Catholics driven from public works, and some
of them beaten, in Ballymacarrett. Shooting, raids
and disorder general over most parts of the city.

26.—Proclamation signed by "competent military
authority" declares illegal an assembly of "three or
more persons" in certain areas of Belfast.

28.—Violent expulsion of Catholic workers from
G.N.R. engine works at Adelaide and Windsor
Stations.

29.—Mr. R. I. Todd (Protestant), proprietor of the
City Bakery, Ardilea Street, writes to the Press
denying the statement that Protestant workers of
the bakery were molested.

* This street adjoins Weaver Street where children were so
atrociously bombed on 13th February, 1922. Several of the
little ones were blown into the air. Nine people seriously
wounded, four of whom were under six years of age. George
Barry, an ex-soldier, was fatally injured. Two houses were
wrecked.

30.—A collection has been taken up in various parts of the city for support and "comforts" for professional Orange gunmen.

September casualties: Eleven dead; fifty-six wounded.

OCTOBER.

3.—Much indignation felt by Catholic residents of Smithfield area at the appearance of lorry of police outside St. Stephen's Protestant Church in Millfield, under pretence that the worshippers attending that church were in danger of attack from Catholic residents. The only conceivable reason for such uncalled for display would seem to be a desire to discredit the residents. No Protestant church or worshippers had ever been interfered with in this locality.

5.—Orange attack on Conway Street Catholic school. Female teacher and two children wounded with stones hurled through windows. Arrival of police and military scatters the mob.

5.—Bomb thrown into house of Mr. Francis Regan (Catholic), 15, Great George's Street, fails to explode.

6.—Conway Street Catholic school closed owing to danger to teachers and children.

7.—Armed raiders rob seven shops belonging to Catholics. One of them, Mr. Reynolds of Lawther Street, had a narrow escape, being fired at after putting up his hands.

14.—Another bomb into Seaforde Street. Does not explode. Belfast pogrom denounced by Belfast Protestants at Labour meeting in Trafalgar Square, London. Children of Richardson Street School (Catholic) several times attacked of late, being guarded by police.

14.—Sir William Allen at an Orange meeting at Portadown, reported as having said: "Ulster had not taken action, but she had not been asleep. She had kept her temper, etc."

14.—Several raids and robberies reported.

19.—More shooting. Three wounded, including Constable Kelly. The constable had arrested an Orange rowdy and was conveying him to Henry Street

Barracks when he was attacked by a mob who tried to rescue the prisoner.

19.—Holds-up and robberies continue.

20—31.—Fairly quiet, but many raids and robberies.

October casualties: Nobody reported killed; about twenty more or less seriously wounded.

NOVEMBER.

12.—Four Orange rowdies charged before Mr. Gray, R.M., with riotous behaviour, singing a ribald song in which the Pope is cursed and giving very great provocation. Fined 40s. each.

18.—*Irish Bulletin* exposes secret police circular, signed by Colonel Wickham, to create a sectarian army of Orangemen in Ulster on Black and Tan lines (see p. 83).

18.—Another fierce onslaught this evening on Catholic residents of Ballymacarrett, and especially on the church, presbytery and convent. It was quite as furious as last year's, though not nearly so successful, owing to the defence put up by the people attacked and the eventual arrival of military and police.

21.—Shooting goes on all day. Only at risk of their lives could Catholics venture out of doors over large areas of the city. **An Orange murderer,** carrying a rifle in broad daylight, walked openly into a public-house in Station Street, Ballymacarrett, shot the barman, James Hogan (twenty-two) dead, then walked out leisurely and joined his companions.

Many wounded, but only three dead to-day.

22.—*Northern Government takes over Powers of Law and Order.*—A terrible day. Three Catholic merchants murdered in their own shops. Orange mob attack St. Matthew's Church and burn down the sexton's house inside the grounds. While thus engaged a bomb was landed in their midst, killing one and wounding forty-five. Workman's tram, containing pogromists from the shipyards, was bombed in Corporation Street in the evening. Two were killed and several injured.

The day's casualties were fifteen killed, eighty-three dangerously wounded and several others less seriously hurt.

23.—Another bad day. Five killed and twenty-five wounded.

23.—British Government repudiates the secret circular. Sir James Craig orders its withdrawal, but——

24.—Another tram bombed. Two killed and eight wounded. Murder gangs still active. Five killed and a dozen wounded in this day's work.

24.—*A pathetic case.*—Mrs. Millar (Catholic), Dock Lane, dead to-day from gunshot wounds, had been wounded in a previous outbreak. In June her son was dragged out of his own house and shot dead. A daughter lost an eye through a bomb explosion. Another daughter was shot in the thigh. A brother had his hand blown off by a bomb explosion.

24.—On hearing of the death of some Protestants by bomb explosion, Sir James Craig wired from London a message to the citizens: " I have learned with the greatest horror of the dastardly outrages made against loyalists in the city of Belfast. I am taking drastic action at once, etc."

(See page 137 for the facts regarding bombing outrages in Belfast up to date).

25.—Murder gangs still at work. Another Catholic merchant killed in his shop.

Total of deaths: Four; of wounded, 20.

29.—*Mother of eight.*—Mrs. McNamara, 56, Keegan Street, mother of eight children, murdered by Orangemen. She died in great agony.

November casualties: Thirty dead; 142 wounded.

DECEMBBER.

6.—Catholic child, four months old, shot in the arms of its mother, Mrs. Valente, confectioner, 10, Castlereagh Road, by one of a gang of about twenty Orange hooligans.

17—18.—Wild week-end in Ballymacarrett. Catholic streets attacked with great ferocity. Three killed and fifteen admitted to hospital. On Saturday five men entered a Catholic shop on Ravenhill Road, and, not finding her husband at home, deliberately shot Mrs. Donnelly, wife of the proprietor, in the abdomen. This woman died a couple of days later.

17—18.—In searching houses in Ballymacarrett, Special Police behaved in a very blackguardly manner, brow-beating females, throwing prayer-books into the fire, smashing and burning sacred objects.

19.—Orange mobs carry service rifles under eyes of Crown forces in Ballymacarrett. Catholic houses looted. Furniture taken out and burned.

19.—Charles MacCallion (Catholic), a barman, murdered at the corner of Brown Street. Hugh Kelly, another barman, seriously injured.

27.—David Morrison, a Catholic ex-soldier, murdered, with six bullets in his head, on Oldpark Road. Said to have been the work of Special Police.

Casualties for December: Seven dead; twenty-three wounded.

TOTAL VICTIMS.

1920—Killed	...	...	**73**
„ **Wounded**	...	...	**395**
1921—Killed	...	...	**130**
„ **Wounded**	...	...	**639**

Total to date: 205 killed; 1,034 wounded.

The name, address and religious persuasion, as far as ascertainable, of each person killed, with date of the occurrence, will be found on pages 159 to 174.

The foregoing summary presents as briefly and as fairly as possible the chief incidents in a long and loathsome period of murder, riot and general disorder. That the activity was not confined altogether to one side will be readily admitted. But an impartial investigation of each notable outbreak would show—as those who were on the spot know well—that the Orange party were, in at least nine cases out of ten, the aggressors. The other side, finding themselves in most instances without any adequate military or police protection, hit back as best they could in self-defence, and often managed to give as much almost as they got. But the great majority of the casualties among the '' loyalists '' were due to the fire of the military and R.I.C.

As in all cases of civic disorder, a large number of the victims were quite innocent people who had taken no active part in the disturbances. That many harmless and respectable Protestants, who had no sympathy with attacks on Catholics, suffered by death or wounding, the writer would be one of the first to admit and deplore.

OUTPOSTS UNDER SIEGE.

ANY summary gives but a very pale reflex of the long-drawn-out agony through which the minority in Belfast have passed in the course of the last twelve months. The tragedies and terrors of many a little street during that period would supply material for more than one sad volume. North

Queen Street has been for nearly all that time a
battleground. The Marrowbone has been subjected
to violent maulings.

ONE AGAINST TEN.

BUT who shall ever write the history of the isolated
Catholic group in Ballymacarrett, surrounded by
coarse, savage enemies in numbers ten to one, well-
armed, confident, and often supported by the forces
of the law !   For a year-and-a-half already that
devoted Catholic area has been living day and night
under an almost unbroken siege.   The inhabitants
are in peril, both indoors and out of doors.   Their
streets are constantly raked and tortured with gun-
fire from the mobs, and from the Special Police.
The throbbing of a police lorry is often but a sure
sign that murder is abroad.   They have seen their
church stoned and peppered by rifle fire half-a-
dozen times at least ; they have seen two attempts
to burn their convent over the heads of the poor
nuns.   Even their priests have been fired at, and
their presbytery several times riddled with bullets:
And the seeming hopelessness of it all as things
grow daily worse and worse ! One victim's funeral
follows another, sometimes three, four or five in
a day.   One wonders over and over again why
they have not all become insane.   And yet they
live and face the future bravely, hopeful of a better
time.

A BOY'S AGONY.

SEVERAL of those wounded went through agonies almost too shocking to contemplate. Here is the case of Thomas Ward, a boy of seventeen, mentioned rather as a type of hundreds of savageries as bad or even worse.

When going home, and not far from his own house on the Woodstock Road, he was surrounded by an Orange gang of over twenty in the midst of a region where the Protestants are at least 200 to 1. They knocked him down on the street and proceeded to kick him most savagely on head, face and body. The poor boy cried out for help, but of course there was no one near to help. A member of the crowd produced a clasp knife, and stabbed him deeply in the back twice. Blood poured from the wounds, but the assailants continued to kick him until he became unconscious. Thinking he was dead, they dragged him into an entry and left him there. On recovering consciousness, he crawled out, and, between falling and rising again, managed to reach the Albert Bridge Road, where a couple of girls, taking pity on his plight, went and informed the police, who had him removed to the Mater Hospital. One of the stabs in the back penetrated the lung, causing a heavy hæmorrhage.

KICKED TO DEATH.

THERE have been several cases of Catholics kicked to death by gangs of Orangemen; never a case of the reverse. Such was the fate of Hugh McDonald, 5 Saul Street, after having been dragged off a tramcar near Queen's Bridge on May 20th, 1922. The writer has witnessed more than one sight of an individual attacked thus by a mob in the streets of Belfast, and has seen several unfortunate victims after a gruelling of this kind, and he can say that anything more horrible could not well be imagined.

With hardly an exception, the Orangeman will not show fight unless he has very strong backing. It is in places in Belfast, where he is in a majority of ten to one, that over 90 per cent. of the outrages on Catholics have been perpetrated. And he has ever been the same.

1,000 versus 1.—Some of the "heroic" performances of the Orange crowds would be utterly incredible to people outside "Ulster." Here is one for which we submit proof that will not be questioned:

After the expulsions of all Catholics from the shipyards of Workman and Clark in *1912*—mark the date—a solitary Papist, a ship-carpenter named Delahunt, ventured into the works one day to get some unclaimed wages lying to his credit in the office. He was spotted. A rush was made for him from all sides. He was knocked down and kicked into pulp.

Some time afterwards this incident was referred to in the course of an action for libel brought against the *Belfast Telegraph* in connection with the expelled shipyard workers. The case was tried in the Four Courts, Dublin, and amongst the witnesses subpoenaed by the plaintiffs to give evidence on that occasion was Superintendent Johnston, an ultra Protestant, head of the Harbour Police, an almost purely Protestant body.

Examined by Mr. Serjeant Moriarty, counsel for the plaintiffs, Mr. Johnston, on oath, stated that he was present with a number of his men, and witnessed the Orange attack on the solitary ship-carpenter.

"How many," said Mr. Moriarty, "would you say were in the crowd that attacked Delahunt?"

"About one thousand," replied Superintendent Johnston.

A CRY AT WESTMINSTER.

THE triple murders of Alexander McBride, William Kerr and Malachy Halfpenny, all three Catholics, during Curfew in the early hours of the 1st June, 1921, caused a feeling of horror in Belfast. The following, from the report of the subsequent raising of the question in the British House of Commons, may interest some people :

" Mr. Devlin, at Westminster, raised the question of Belfast atrocities, and especially of the slaughter of innocent men during Curfew hours.

" On September 26th," he said, " in the early hours of Sunday morning, armed and uniformed men, wearing uniform caps, drove out to the house of a man called Edward Trodden in Falls Road, and there, in the presence of his wife and children, dragged him out into the back yard and murdered him. They proceeded to the house of John Gaynor in Springfield Road, forced their way into the house, and they did this young man to death in the presence of his aged mother. They then proceeded to the house of John McFadden, Springfield Road, and they murdered him.

He referred to the case of the two brothers Duffin, shot in their home after midnight on Sunday, April 24th.

Then he referred to the similar murders of McBride, Kerr, and Halfpenny on the previous Sunday.

" McBride was but a year married, with a wife and one child. He belonged to no political organisation of any kind.

" Kerr was a constitutionalist, and his brother was a regimental sergeant in the army.

" Halfpenny, a youth of 22, who had fought in the British Army for three-and-a-half years, where

he was twice wounded and once gassed, was taken
from his bed practically naked, driven away and murdered.   His body was riddled with bullets.

"An Hon. Member: 'The dirty dogs.'

"Major Prescott: 'Does the hon. gentleman wish
the House to believe that servants of the Crown put
an end to such a life as that?'

"Mr. Devlin said that after 10.30 p.m. no civilian
and no motor cars were allowed on the streets of
Belfast.   Who but the Forces of the Crown could have
rampaged the whole city at one o'clock in the morning, stopped at three houses and murdered men in
the presence of their families—leaving them lying
dead until Curfew was over in the morning?

"Sir Hamar Greenwood replied, with regard to
Mr. Devlin's remarks, that it was unworthy to assume
that any of those murders was committed by servants who were upholding the authority of the House
in the country.

"Mr. Devlin: 'Were they brave men who murdered Canon Magner?'

"Sir Hamar Greenwood: 'No'."

HOW CURFEW WAS CARRIED OUT.

THOUGH, as all the evidence makes clear, and as
the representatives of the British and foreign Press
have amply testified, the aggression was at first
entirely, and afterwards chiefly, on the part of the
anti-Catholic elements, the authorities acted all
along just as if the opposite were the fact.   But
such has been the traditional method in Belfast.

The manner in which Curfew has been carried
out is a good example of this.   The Catholic district of Falls Road (one of the most peaceful areas
in these islands, until the visits of the Special Constabulary produced trouble there) was, from the

first imposition of the Curfew order, made the constant and special object of military activity by night and every night ; whilst the Protestant areas were practically left to take care of themselves, except for the rare passing of a military car or lorry. Numberless raids and searches were carried out in Catholic homes.   These unfortunate people could never promise themselves half-an-hour's rest, whilst the worst malefactors of another creed were allowed to sleep undisturbed.   Those senseless raids, as those who carried them out well know, hardly ever resulted in anything except the great annoyance of the poor people thus helplessly afflicted.   It must have been little less annoying and disgusting to the military—who, as a rule, carried out their orders with courtesy and consideration—to be nightly and hourly engaged grubbing, delving, raking and " combing " in the houses of these poor people, until the whole Catholic community might be said to have been put through a sieve, not once, but several times.   And what did they succeed in finding ?   Practically nothing at all, or something that might make a cat laugh.

The victims of this senseless activity never blamed the military.   They felt such work was repugnant to most of them, and rather sympathised with them.   But they suspected that those responsible for issuing such orders had allowed themselves, quite unconsciously, no doubt, to be made the tools of a malignant faction.

"CATHOLICS THEMSELVES TO BLAME FOR POGROM!"

SOME people with wonderfully short memories have been found of late to express the view that the Catholics of Belfast and environs have only themselves to blame for the horrors that exist there ; that the trouble is chiefly due to the fact that they refused to recognise the Northern Parliament. The case is put very ingenuously thus :

A Government was established for the southern twenty-six counties.   Such an arrangement was, of course, distasteful to the Protestants of that area, nevertheless they acquiesced without hesitation and declared their allegiance to it.   Should not the Catholics of the six counties have acted similarly towards the new Government there ?   Their attitude of opposition has led to all this trouble, etc., etc.

To many people it will seem childish to stop to deal with arguments of this kind.   But it is well to assume that people who talk thus are sincere in their view, however astonishing the ignorance such views connote.   The facts put forward in the earlier portion of this book, ought to make it clear to them that their contention has no foundation whatever to rest upon.

THIS PICTURE.

THE Government formed for the South came into being in January of the present year.   The

Protestants, in tendering their allegiance to the New State, could recall the consoling fact that they were throwing in their lot with fellow-countrymen of a different creed who, according to the abounding testimony of the Protestants themselves, had for ages treated them with the utmost fairness and brotherliness. Their religion, or even their known political views, had never been made a reason for hostility or exclusion in any form. In many ways they had been given what might be described as preferential treatment by the Catholics among whom they lived. These points need not be pressed farther.

AND THIS.

IN June, 1921, the Government of the Six Counties was called into existence. *Already for practically a whole year, the Catholics of Belfast and of many other places had been suffering at the hands of those who now demanded their allegiance and co-operation the agonies of a wholesale persecution such as no Christians in any part of the world outside Turkey have been subjected to in modern times.* And this was only the latest of a long series, periodically inflicted upon them, simply on account of their religion and national sentiment, by the same party of bigots and national parricides. The Premier of the New Government had gone out of his way, a few months before, to assure the very men who had driven thousands of Catholics per-

manently from the work that gave them and theirs
a living, who had been active in works of murder,
wounding, looting, burning, convent sacking and
church wrecking, that he fully approved of what
they had done. Most of the other members of the
Government had records of fierce bigotry. The
Parliament, in the eyes of any northern Catholic,
could appear little else than a glorified Orange
Lodge.

A fine parallel this, surely, between the case of
the southern Protestants and that of the northern
Catholics yielding allegiance to the respective
Governments !

THE NATIONAL SENTIMENT.

BUT the consideration of national sentiment in-
volved shows such a comparison to be still more
absurd. The Protestants of the North-East have
always proclaimed that they are as Irish as any
others in the land, and no one wishes to quarrel
with such professions. What hardship then is
offered to them in asking them to remain and com-
port themselves as citizens of their native land?
Do they fear persecution at the hands of the
Catholic minority? Let the reader consult the
testimony from many recent Protestant sources
found towards the end of this volume (p. 186)
and then judge for himself as to such an attitude.

But to every one of the hundreds of thousands
of Catholics in Carsonia such a violent and un-

natural severance from the rest of the Irish nation is of the nature of a tragedy too deep for utterance. The Protestants say that they themselves never asked for such separation. The Catholics have abhorred it, and will for ever oppose it, not out of a dislike of the Protestant "Ulsterites," but from pure love of Ireland, which England, the old enemy, would rend in twain for her own sinister political designs.

WICKHAM SECRET CIRCULAR

"Divisional Commissioner's Office,
"R.I.C., Belfast,
"9th Nov., 1921.

"Secret.

"Commissioners.

"All County Commandants.

"Owing to the number of reports which has been received as to the growth of unauthorised loyalist defence forces, the Government have under consideration the desirability of obtaining the services of the best elements of these organisations.

"They have decided that the scheme most likely to meet the situation would be to enrol all who volunteer and are considered suitable into Class 'C.' and to form them into regular military units.

"The force must be raised on a territorial basis, namely, the county must be divided into battalion areas of such a size as will produce a battalion of, roughly, one thousand men.

"Before proceeding further with the scheme County Commandants, after a consultation with County Inspectors, should report the number of battalion areas for their counties, with a recommendation for the name of the battalion commander. At this stage proposed battalion commanders should not be approached as to their willingness to undertake the duty; all that is required is the nomination of the men who are considered to be the most suitable.

"If it is necessary to form this force it will have to be done on very short notice, which means that the battalion commanders, once appointed, will have to be given a free hand to raise and organise their men. It is necessary, therefore, that those appointed should be men of military experience and organising ability.

"The force is intended as a military one only, to be called out in grave emergency, to act in a military capacity. They will not of necessity be utilised for local defence, but may be drafted to any theatres of operations within the six counties.

"It is not intended that this force should interfere with or replace Class 'B.' Special Constabulary, who remain a local force for local protection. There is no objection to an officer of Class 'B.' being appointed an officer to Class 'C.' if he is considered the most suitable, and if a deputy is available to carry on his 'B.' duties.

"The 'C.' scheme, therefore, applies mostly to towns and cities where there is a population surplus to 'B.' requirements. The most suitable class for this force are ex-soldiers, who possess already the necessary military training and knowledge of arms.

"As the matter is URGENT, replies should be sent at the earliest possible date. Further details as to pay when called out, arms, drilling, recruiting, etc. will be considered and notified as soon as the general idea is received as to the umber of battalions which can be raised. There is no necessity to endeavour to produce the maximum possible number of units; what is required is to ensure that every unit recommended for formation can be constituted from a reliable section of the population.

         "(Signed),

               "WICKHAM, Lieut.-Colonel,

                  "Divisional Commissioner."

THE PLOT EXPOSED.

" IT would be invidious at such a moment,"
says the *Irish Bulletin,* " to question the sincerity
of the British Government in its search for peace.
A document has, however, come into our possession
which will cause the gravest concern. The facts
disclosed in it are of a sinister character and, if the
interpretation we place upon them in the detailed
analysis which follows is correct, it is difficult to
avoid the conclusion that a step has been deliberately taken to wreck any possibility of peace. An
army is being secretly organised in North-East
Ulster—organised, as the document admits, by the
British Government—with the apparent object of
taking the field at any given moment, and thus providing an excuse for its organisers to abandon any
settlement that may be come to at the Conference.

SEQUENCE OF EVENTS.

" THE document in question is dated November
9th. On November 5th Sir James Craig, leader
of the Ulster Unionists, arrived in London from
Belfast.   He declared that he came ' on private
business only,' and four hours later he was closeted
with Mr. Lloyd George, and subsequently called on
Lord Carson, organiser of the Ulster Volunteer
Force. On November 7th Sir James Craig again
saw the British Premier and that evening summoned
his Cabinet to London. On November 8th an
official announcement by Sir James Craig stated

' he had spent another strenuous day in consultation with various (British) Government officials '
and later he again interviewed Mr. Lloyd George.
On November 9th the foregoing circular was
issued.''

DETAILED ANALYSIS.

HAS THE MOVE BEEN MADE BY GOVERNMENT AUTHORITY?

'' LET us,'' proceeds the *Bulletin,* '' analyse this
grave circular paragraph by paragraph.

'' Par. 1 states that the orders to create this
secret army came from the British Government,
a fact already indicated by its issue from the office
of the British Divisional Commissioner of Constabulary in Belfast. The character of the army
is laid down in this first paragraph as definitely
sectarian. It is to be enrolled exclusively from
' the best elements ' of the unauthorised loyalist
(*i.e.* Protestant) defence forces which have already
been created to defeat the present peace negotiations.

'' Par. 2 outlines the general scheme of organisation. The Class ' C ' referred to is a branch of the
Ulster Special Constabulary whose main function
hitherto has been to join in pogroms upon the
Nationalist minority in Belfast and elsewhere. The
members of this class were restrained to a slight
degree by the name they bore. As ' police ' they

could not carry on their work of persecution as openly as they would have wished. They are now to be reorganised as ' military units,' their numbers are to be increased by ' all who volunteer and are considered suitable,' and the mild restraint of their position as constabulary is to be abolished.

" Unlimited Strength.

" Par. 3 indicates that the army is to be of unlimited strength. This paragraph further suggests that the force to be raised is to be an army whose members will live in their own homes. This will ensure a lack of discipline, a freedom for ' unauthorised ' action, and unlimited opportunity to attack the local Nationalist minority, all of which were doubtless foreseen and appreciated by the organisers of the army.

" Par. 4 makes it certain that the officers who are to command the new force will be of the right political colour. They must first be approved by the County Commandants of the Ulster Special Constabulary and the County Inspectors of the Royal Irish Constabulary, all of whom are either members of the extreme Orange section or bitter opponents of the Nationalist minority. But the County Commandants or County Inspectors have not the power of appointment. They may nominate, but the final selection is evidently to be made in consultation with Sir James Craig and his colleagues who may be relied upon to weed out any

weaklings suggested by their Constabulary sup-
porters. This paragraph instances the caution
with which the secret army is being raised. Even
the nominated commanders are to know nothing of
the scheme until they have been vetted and passed
by the inner Orange circle.

" Underlying Motive.

" Par. 5 shows that the underlying motive of the
scheme is political. ' If it is necessary ' the force
will be formed ' on very short notice.' Then the.
force is not yet necessary. Its necessity depends
apparently upon some impending political contingency. Such political contingency can arise only
out of the present negotiations. If a settlement
seems on the point of being come to, ' short notice'
may be given and the force spring into immediate
existence. A more extensive Curragh mutiny will
thus have been effectively staged. ' Ulster ' will
seemingly have risen as one man. (NOTE.—The
circular is marked ' Secret '; the public were to
have known nothing of the new army until the
moment of a ' spontaneous rising ' had come). In
such an eventuality will the British Government act
as it acted in 1914 and under the seeming compul-
sion of circumstances (which it had itself secretly
arranged) abandon its own proposals? This paragraph also states that the British Commanders,
having been duly passed as politically sound, will
be ' given a free hand.' The Auxiliary Cadets

were ' given a free hand ' ; so were the Black and Tans.

A MILITARY ONE ONLY.

No Plea of Preserving Law and Order Needed.

" Par. 6 declares that the force is intended ' as a military one only.' The implication is that they can begin operations without any contributing cause on the part of those they intend to assail ; they will simply obey instructions and need not advance the plea of ' preserving law and order.' This paragraph also suggests that when the word is given, the army will concentrate on the Nationalist counties of Tyrone and Fermanagh, or homogeneous Nationalist districts, such as South Armagh, North Antrim, South and East Down, etc.

" Par. 7 indicates that the secret army is to be an addition to, not a replacement of, the existing sectarian forces in North-East Ulster. The army may thus safely be concentrated in any one district, leaving the Nationalist minorities in the other districts still under the heel of the Special Constabulary.

" The Secret Army.

" Par. 8 emphasises this point further. The active branches of the Special Constabulary are to continue at full strength. It is the ' surplus

D

population ' which is to be enrolled as the secret
army. This paragraph also provides the information that the army is to be modelled on the lines of
the Black and Tans   It is to be made up of ex-
soldiers, brutalised by the Great War, and recruited
from the cities and towns where sectarianism is
more rampant than in the country districts, just
as the unemployed in English cities and towns were
formed into ' Royal Irish Constables.' This has
also a bearing on the Belfast labour question which
is beginning to endanger the stability of the
Northern Government. The sweated workers and
the unemployed are to have their attention directed
away from their treatment by the capitalist classes.

" Disappearing Force.

" Par. 9 repeats that the matter is of great
urgency. The political need for a ' crisis ' may
arise at any moment. On November 9th the
British Cabinet, according to the Press, were dis-
cussing the position of North-East Ulster, and were
alleged to have come to a unanimous decision. But
this document shows that on that date the British
Government were actually pledged to organise, pay,
train, and instruct an army whose personnel would
ensure opposition to the decisions they were stated
to have arrived at. This paragraph further sup-
ports the point that the army is designed for
political purposes and not to meet any military need.
In the first place, the number of troops required is

not specified. Therefore, there can be no military objective in view. Secondly, the document states that when ' necessary ' the force is to be formed ' at short notice.' Therefore, a disciplined military campaign is not in contemplation, but, rather, something like a disappearing army which will jump to arms whenever such action is calculated to overawe, or seem to overawe, some politician. Thirdly, the army is to be selected not from the physically strongest part of the people, but from the most ' reliable section of the population '—in other words, from the extremists. Political reliability is the only test of membership and the only limitation placed upon number.

. . . .

" It may be that this secret circular calling into existence an army selected for its hatred of the minority, upon whom it is to be quartered, was issued without the knowledge of the British Government. But the terms and the origin of the circular do not bear out that view. A full explanation is obviously necessary, the more so as this official formation of a sectarian army is taking place during the Truce, the terms of which are gravely infringed by it."

This premature exposure of their plans arrested the movement—for the time—and Sir James Craig sent the following telegram to the Minister for Home Affairs of the " Northern Parliament " :

"My attention has been drawn to the terms of Colonel Wickham's circular of November 9, with regard to the recruiting Class 'C.' of the Special Constabulary, which I approved in the event of the Truce being terminated, but for their formation into a regular military unit the Constabulary has never been transferred to the Government of Northern Ireland.

"The recruits may be taken as police, but not into a military force for organisation.

"I am returning on Saturday morning, when I will explain the legal position.

"Meanwhile the circular must be withdrawn."

SAMPLES OF ORANGE LOYALTY

In another section of this work the preposterous claim to an eminent loyalty on the part of the Orangemen is considered at some length. It may not be out of place to adduce a few instances here out of many of the same kind witnessed during the outbreaks of the past two years. The following incident took place on 16th October, 1920:

KICKING THE KING'S UNIFORM.

A Protestant family had kindly taken into their house trunks belonging to a Catholic neighbour whose house had been burned. They were warned by the Orange faction that if they did not get rid of them the house would be burned over their heads. The police were informed, and eventually two men offered to remove the trunks if police protected them. The men were Francis McNeill, of 39, Gracehill Street, an ex-soldier, and Private Francis Scullion, of the 2nd Battalion Black Watch, who was home on leave. Whilst placing the trunks on a handcart they were surrounded by an Orange mob. McNeill was stabbed in the back of the head, grew faint and fell, and was then savagely kicked. Private Scullion was knocked down by a blow of a large stone, and, though dressed in the King's uniform, was brutally kicked as he lay. One bystander ventured to cry " Shame ; you should not a beat a man in khaki," but this had no effect on the mob. Finally the two unfortunate men were rescued. A running fight with revolvers followed between the three policemen and the Orange mob, until an armoured car arrived and drove the latter off helter skelter.

A LETTER FROM THE KING.

ON 13th June, 1921, Mrs. Kerr of 42, Vere Street, received a letter from King George V. accompanied by a bronze plaque in memory of her husband, who had made the supreme sacrifice for Britain in the Great War. Within an hour after the receipt of this royal message her house was furiously attacked by an Orange gang and partially wrecked. Mrs. Kerr, it need hardly be added, was a Catholic.

On June 20th, 1921, Patrick O'Hare of Urney Street, a soldier in the Connaught Rangers, home on furlough and in uniform, was, with his wife and small children, evicted by an Orange mob, who dragged him out and threatened to shoot him if he refused to clear off. He returned to his regiment, leaving his family homeless behind him in loyal Belfast.

BRITISH SOLDIERS KILLED AND WOUNDED.

IN several authenticated instances soldiers of English regiments doing duty on the streets in Belfast were deliberately shot at and killed or wounded by Orange crowds. Such instances could be multiplied indefinitely, but the foregoing may be sufficient to indicate the kind of loyalty obtaining in Protestant Belfast, where close on two thousand Catholic ex-service men have been expelled from their employment, driven forth to meet starvation, and compelled ever since to live on the world's charity by Belfast loyalists.

THIRD YEAR, 1922

LAW AND ORDER UNDER THE BELFAST PARLIAMENT

To realise fully the significance of events since the beginning of 1922 it is necessary to bear in mind the fact that the Belfast Government was now placed in control of " law and order " in the Six Counties. The transference of the police to the Belfast Government, persistently clamoured for since the opening of the Belfast Parliament, had at last been acceded to by the British Cabinet ready to humour the whims of its Belfast proteges. What the consequences of such a step were bound to be could not escape the veriest political simpleton. The use to which the Belfast Government intended to put its new powers had been made sufficiently clear by the Wickham circular of November. The Home Office, which was henceforth to administer " law and order " in the Six County area, was in charge of a notorious anti-Catholic bigot, Sir Dawson Bates. His bigotry was his chief qualification for this office.

THE " BOYS."

SIR JAMES CRAIG had, as we have already seen
(14th October, 1920), expressed his warm approval
of the action of " you, boys " in expelling the
Catholics from the shipyards and other places of
employment.   Thousands of these " boys " had
already been enrolled in the Special Constabulary
by the authority and under the control of the
British Government.   But the Wickham circular and speeches by Sir James Craig in
recent months show that it was the intention
of the Belfast Cabinet, as soon as it was invested
with full powers, to enrol these same " boys " and
others of their ilk, not in their thousands but in their
tens of thousands.   This has already been done.
Fifty thousand Special Constabulary supplemented
by remnants of the old R.I.C. and by new forma-
tions of what is proposed to be the future permanent
police of the Six Counties—the Royal Ulster
Constabulary—now exercise throughout Ulster, in
its cities and towns, its remote villages and glens,
a Terror perhaps occasionally equalled but never
surpassed by the worst phases of Black-and-
Tannery.   In many respects indeed it is infinitely
worse, and more thorough.   During the Greenwood Terror the total of police in all Ireland never
reached more than 19,000 (?) in addition to
60,000 (?) British soldiers.   That is 79,000 armed
men to a population of 4,500,000.   To-day in Six
Counties of Ulster there are 50,000 armed police,.

supported by 20,000 British soldiers, that is, a total of 70,000 armed men to a population of 1,200,000, or 1 to every 17 inhabitants l

THEIR QUALIFICATIONS.

FOR exercising a Terror these men are in a much better position than were the Black-and-Tans. They are local men, recruited for the most part from the dregs of society, brought up from their earliest years in an atmosphere of anti-Catholic bigotry, taught both by their political and religious leaders that their Catholic neighbours are their only enemy, and inflamed by the subtle innuendoes and brazen lies of the most malignant Press in the world. Such are the instruments employed by the Government of Belfast to carry out the traditional policy of that Government's master, the Orange Lodge, viz., the evacuation and extermination of the Catholics from Ulster.

SIR JAMES CRAIG STILL ASKS FOR MORE.

YET Sir James Craig is not satisfied with the progress made by this instrument of diabolic efficiency. In a recent speech he asserted that their police system was so devised as to enable the entire body of " loyal " men in Ulster to arm themselves. In other words he was aiming at the arming of the whole Protestant population against their Catholic neighbours. English policy in Ulster at least made a pretence of " keeping the ring," to use the

elegant expression used by Lord Fitzalan at the
opening of the Belfast Parliament.   The Belfast
Government makes no pretence about its aims.   It
has no use for any cant about " keeping the ring."
It has deliberately unchained forces whose one
simple object is the extermination of the Catholic
population in the Six Counties.   The rioting mob,
the snipers, the murder gang, and the Special
Constabulary are not so many distinct institutions
of Belfast life ;   they are all parts of the same
organism ;   or, rather, they are one and the same
set of forces operating in different ways.   Owing
to the ingenious system of A., B. and C. Specials,
individuals can operate in some or all of the four
above-mentioned capacities within the space of a
few hours.   And it is a mere truism to state the
fact, of which everyone in Belfast is aware, that the
Specials supply with arms and ammunition the
mobs, the snipers, and the murder gangs in whose
activities the Specials take a very prominent part.

THE MACHINE AT WORK

JANUARY 1st to 21st.

DURING the first five days of January there occurred five bomb outrages, in each case the bomb
being hurled either into a Catholic quarter or into
a Catholic house.   There was fierce rioting in York
Street area, followed by the imposition of 8 o'clock

Curfew in that area, and the relaxation of Curfew in the Orange area of Ballymacarrett, whereupon the Orange mob, becoming as aggressive as ever, again attacked in force St. Matthew's Church with rifle fire.

BABIES SHOT.

DURING the riot in the York Street area an infant was shot dead in its mother's arms by an Orange gunman, and another child in Kilmood Street was wounded in the face. In all there were eight deaths during these five days and many wounded.

AND A SOLDIER OF THE KING.

AMONG the dead was Private Barnes, shot openly by an Orange gunman, and Alex. Twittle, an Orange sniper of whose death the following official report was issued :

" A soldier was sniped at. He returned the fire and shot the sniper dead."

On the night of the 3rd it has been estimated that the military fired 20,000 rounds in York Street area, whilst in Ballymacarrett the Orange mob was throwing bombs and attacking St. Matthew's Church with impunity.

At an inquest on some of the victims of recent massacres a rider was added to the verdict that " no effective measures had been taken by the responsible authorities for the preservation of the peace." This rider expressed only a half-truth.

In view of the machinery of " law and order " out-lined above, a fuller realisation of the situation would have found expression in something like these terms, that " the most effective measures had been taken by the responsible authorities to ensure continuous breaches of the peace." As we have seen before, even English newspapers like *The Times* and *Daily Mail* had foreseen as much months previously when the question of establishing a force of Special Constabulary from the Ulster Volunteer Force was first mooted.

"CATHOLIC AGGRESSIVENESS."

ON January 6th there were inquests on nineteen victims of recent disturbances, seventeen of whom were Catholic ; and one of the two Protestants had been shot in a Catholic shop, undoubtedly having been taken for a Catholic. And yet, in spite of the eloquence of such figures, the Belfast Orange Press repeats *ad nauseam* the hoary lie that the Catholics are the aggressors !

The conditions during the next few weeks, until the 21st January, the date of the first Collins-Craig Pact, are just a continuation of those described as prevailing during the opening days of the month—rioting, sniping, murder, bombing, firing into Catholic districts by the military by way of reply to Orange attacks. Such is the history of Belfast at this time. The results of these activities were nine persons killed, four of whom were women.

Three of these women were Catholics deliberately murdered on their doorsteps. And there were large numbers of wounded. During these weeks the murder gangs were operating with extraordinary boldness, frequently claiming their victims in broad daylight. The majority of those killed and wounded were the victims of these operations. On the 12th January inquests were held on seven people of whom six were Catholics. Total deaths since January 1st, 16.

Once again at this time was it shown that the pogrom had the blessing of the Belfast Parliament and Government. Mr. Moles, in a speech in Parliament, with the approval of his colleagues, outlined a scheme whereby Catholics might be got rid of by a process of evacuation.

THE COLLINS-CRAIG PACT AND ITS FATE.

JANUARY 21st to END OF FEBRUARY.

ON January 21st the terms of an agreement signed by Mr. Collins and Sir James Craig relative to the situation in Ulster were published. It consisted of five clauses. No. 1 dealt with the boundary question ; No. 3 with the settlement of the railway dispute ; No. 4 with the Council of Ireland ; No. 5 made provision for a subsequent meeting of the signatories to deal with the case of post-truce prisoners.

BOYCOTT OF BELFAST REMOVED.

CLAUSE No. 2, which has the most direct bearing upon the Catholic position in Belfast, deserves to be quoted in full It is as follows :

" Without prejudice to the future consideration by his Government on the question of tariffs, Mr. Collins undertakes that the Belfast boycott is to be discontinued immediately, and Sir James Craig undertakes to facilitate in every possible way the return of Catholic workmen without tests to the shipyards, as and when trade revival enables the firms concerned to absorb the present unemployed. In the meantime a system of relief on a large scale is being arranged to carry over the period of distress."

Now, here was a clause which, if honourably carried out, or if even a serious attempt had been made to carry it out, would have gone far to ease the whole situation, particularly in Belfast which is the canker spot of the whole Ulster situation. As everyone knows, the expulsion of the Catholics from their work, either by the direct application of violence, or indirectly by the attempted imposition of impudent religious and political tests, was the reason for the imposition by Southern Ireland of the boycott on Belfast goods. Mr. Collins immediately after the signing of the Pact fulfilled his undertaking and the boycott was lifted.

SIR JAMES CRAIG FAILS TO MAKE GOOD.

HAD Sir James Craig had the will and the courage to honour his signature in the same way, Belfast might have been spared the months of carnage

which have since supervened   Let us suppose that
he had the will, then we are driven to the conclusion
that he had not the courage to enforce his will. Nor
is this mere speculation.   The master-pogromists
of the shipyards interposed their veto.   On January
30th a secret meeting was held in Workman and
Clark's yard and a resolution was passed that the
men " would not work with any Papists."   In
acting thus, these men were showing themselves
more logical than Sir James Craig.   They had
already received Sir James' approval of their action
in expelling the Catholics, and they naturally
resented the new orientation of his policy as indicated in the Pact with Mr. Collins.   And to prove
that they meant their resolution to be no empty
vapouring the pogrom was renewed during the
month of February in all its intensity.   The
casualty lists from February 6th till February 25th
were :

	Killed.	
Catholics	...	27
Protestants	...	16

	Wounded.	
Catholics	...	69
Protestants	...	26

But the mere recital of these figures gives no
adequate idea of the Terror.   Dealing with one
day alone the *Northern Whig* had the following
caption : " Black Day in Belfast.   Twelve Dead ;
over Forty Wounded. Murders, Bomb-throwing,
Sniping."

CHILDREN SLAUGHTERED BY BOMB.

IT was on this day that occurred a more horrible outrage than any that had hitherto disgraced this savage city.   Weaver Street is a small Catholic street sandwiched right in the heart of an exclusively Protestant area.   A crowd of the Catholic children of this street were playing here when a bomb was hurled into their midst.   The savagery and callousness of this deed beggar description. Two children were killed outright, several were blown into the air and mangled ; and four others died later in hospital from their wounds.   The Orange bombers of Belfast had evidently taken to heart the words of Cromwell, when he, too, gave orders to spare neither age nor sex ; for, said he, '' nits will be lice.''   Speaking of this outrage in the British House of Commons, Mr. Churchill said : '' *It is the worst thing that has happened in Ireland in the last three years.*''   Several continental papers, however, gave a completely distorted version of Protestants bombed by Sinn Feiners !

A DEAF MUTE.

ANOTHER horrible atrocity was that in which Cecil Smyth, a Catholic deaf mute, was almost beaten to death near his home at New Andrew Street.   On the 14th of February the Press contained the names of another twelve killed and fourteen wounded.

HOW A BOY WAS MURDERED.

THE brutal death meted out to many of the Catholic victims may be illustrated by the following description (officially confirmed) of the murder of James Rice (19), a Catholic resident of Avondale Street. At 9 p.m. he was set upon at Ravenscroft Street by a mob of armed hooligans who knocked him down and kicked him unmercifully. His hands were tied behind his back and he was blindfolded with his own neck-scarf. Thus prostrate, helpless and bleeding, he was fired at and killed as he lay on the ground. Having done him to death, his torturers battered in his skull with their revolvers, pulled his coat over his head, and left his mangled corpse there.

THE OLD STORY.

ONCE again the usual attempts were made to make it appear that it was Catholic aggression that was responsible for this hideous outburst of savagery. Sir James Craig wired Mr. Churchill that " The present outbreak began by shootings in Wall Street, a mixed locality, on Sunday last." But he did not mention that, previous to those shootings, Thomas Gray (19), a young Catholic assistant in Boyle's of Earl Street, had been deliberately murdered in the shop by Orange gunmen. It was this cold-blooded murder, the first serious act in the counter-offensive against the Collins-Craig Pact, and an Orange bombing outrage the same day, that provoked the series of tragedies which ensued.

About the same time as Sir James Craig sent his
lying wire, Most Rev. Dr. MacRory, Catholic
Bishop of Belfast, felt compelled to wire Mr. Lloyd
George about " the lawlessness in Belfast and the
butchery of his people." He protested also
against the inactivity of the British military, who
afforded little or no protection to Catholics against
the Orange mobs and murder-gangs.

COMMONPLACES.

ON February 15th, ten more persons were killed
and seventeen wounded. A Catholic funeral, that of
Mr. Patrick Lambe, recently murdered, was fired
upon from the Orange quarter at Carlisle Circus.
So aggressive did the Orange mob become on this
occasion that they had to be dispersed by military
fire. On the same day Mrs. Brennan, who had
given birth to a baby only a few days previously,
had her house raided and she died as a result of
shock.

CAMOUFLAGED APPROVAL.

As this particular orgy of blood was abating some-
what, the Northern Cabinet, the custodians of
" law and order," congratulated the " loyalists "
of the Six Counties on the great restraint and self-
command shown by them under the strain of outrages recently committed. Has ever any responsible body making a pretence of functioning as a
Government dared to encourage outrage and

murder against a helpless minority in such slightly camouflaged terms of approval? No wonder that the Orange mobs and murder gangs, reading this official approval of their "restraint and self-control," measured by the murder of twenty-seven Catholics and nearly thrice that number wounded, should feel satisfied with themselves and prepare to earn greater approbation from their leaders by the further exercise of this particular form of "restraint." The fact, of course, is that the gang who control the Belfast Parliament and Government have never yet had the faintest glimmerings of their functions as a Government; they are simply the representative of a vindictive, bigoted and fanatical political party who have confounded government with the pursuance of an antiquated and bloody vendetta against the Catholic minority in their midst.

A TIMID ADMISSION.

DIARIST writes in the *Star*, 16th February, 1922 :

"The English papers are being badly served by the Ulster correspondents in the matter of the Belfast murders. There is hardly a word to suggest what appears to be the fact, that what is happening is a sort of Protestant pogrom against the Catholic minority."

Even this correspondent displays considerable hesitancy in facing and making known the very fact to which he refers when he qualifies the Belfast savagery as "a sort of Protestant pogrom against the Catholic minority."

FOR PROTESTANTISM.

THE following incident is highly significant and helps to reveal the forces which rendered the Pact a dead letter on the northern side, assuming that Sir James Craig ever really intended to fulfil his undertaking. Mr. Tregenna, a well-known Orange firebrand employed in one of the shipyards, attended a meeting held at Omagh to protest against any alteration of the Six-County boundary. The presence of Tregenna, brought all the way from the Belfast shipyards to address this meeting, reveals the ramification of a movement, in which the " boys " of the shipyards were the moving spirit, to render not merely Clause 2 but the entire Pact nugatory. Sir James Craig, Lord Londonderry, etc. may sign pacts and express pious hopes, but the real dictators of Belfast policy, and at the same time its executors, are the Orange shipyard workers and their henchmen, the Special Constabulary. Mr. Tregenna was introduced to the Omagh meeting as " the representation of the fighting men of Belfast." " They had enrolled 40,000 men in the Imperial Guards," he said, " to stand by Ulster in spite of Lloyd George and the intriguers—*even of some in the Belfast Parliament.* He was as strong a labour man as any, but he could never find anything strong enough to put forward in Labour to *override the religious question.* The Protestant who did not come into the fight for Protestantism was not worthy of its name."

HIS MASTER'S VOICE.

HERE we have a pronouncement in the straight line of descent from that made by Sir Edward Carson on a previous occasion when he said that the religious aspect of the Ulster question could not be over-emphasised.   The reference to intriguers in the Ulster Parliament was plainly meant as a warning to Sir James Craig to toe the line to his shipyard dictators who had no use for pacts or Papishes.

HOW DEFENDERS OF EMPIRE WERE TREATED.

As an example of how the "fight for Protestantism" was to go on, the disabled Catholic ex-soldiers in Craigavon military hospital, Belfast, were served on February 24th with notices of a very vile kind and ordered to clear out within three days.   Here are the notices :

"If any óf you traitor dogs are got about the place from now look out for what you get.   Death to Rebels and Papists.   Red Hand for ever.   Don't blame men in hospital, but we won't have you among the loyalists."
"You low-bred swine."

A second notice, served under the form of a telegram, couched in still viler terms, gives, with the above, an insight into what " loyalty " means in Belfast, and into the Orangeman's conception of " civil and religious liberty."   Here is the telegram :

"You and your sneaking dogs of Papists must go.

£5 reward won't save yous, nor all Popes, Priests,
Holy Water or Holy Marys. Time's up. Go or we
will riddle every rotten Papist in Craigavon and
U.V.F. hospital, as you are a rotten lot of ———"

Further comment upon this episode is needless
when it is remembered that those to whom these
threatening messages were addressed were invalid
ex-soldiers who had fought for the same King and
Empire to which their persecutors are so fond of
paying tributes of lip-loyalty.   The crime of which
these unfortunate ex-soldiers were guilty was that
of being Catholics.   Needless to add, they cleared
out of the two military hospitals in question, for it
is never safe to disregard the threats of a Belfast
murder-gang.

LAW NO DETERRENT.

THOSE who do not know Belfast may be surprised
that, with all the immense machinery, ostensibly
devised to keep the peace and punish evil-doers, no
one is ever made amenable for the atrocities committed on Catholics.   But those who have read
this book up to this point will have ere now ceased
to wonder at a fact which, to those accustomed to
the normal operations of the law only among
civilised communities, must remain incomprehen-
sible.   Occasionally, perhaps by mistake, an
Orangeman is arrested for murder ; but arrest on
a charge of murdering a Catholic need have no
terrors for the Belfast Orangeman.   He knows
there is hardly the slightest danger of a conviction,

no matter how overwhelming may be the evidence against him. For example, David Duncan, a Protestant, long notorious to Catholic circles as a leading gunman, was charged with the murder of James McIvor, a Catholic shopkeeper. Bernard Monaghan, an ex-soldier, swore that he saw Duncan and another man go to McIvor's door and fire five or six shots which caused McIvor's death. After nine minutes' absence the jury brought in a verdict of " *Not guilty.*" Had Duncan been a Catholic brought up on a charge of murdering a Protestant, and had similar evidence been tendered against him, who that knows the temper and mentality of Belfast juries doubts what his fate would have been ?

During the month of February, armed robberies and the throwing of bombs into Catholic quarters and houses continued, there being at least seven authenticated cases of bombing. A feature of the slaughters at this period is the fact that the number of Catholics murdered in their own homes or shops is on the increase in proportion to the number killed in general street fighting and sniping. This is due to the clearer realisation by the Orange gangs that they can carry on their activities with absolute impunity under the ægis of the Northern Government which unctuously congratulates them on their restraint.

Of course the outrages were not all on one side. Catholics occasionally hit back fiercely enough, but the injuries they inflicted were small compared with what themselves were obliged to suffer.

CRYING IN WILDERNESS.

IN the midst of this scene of a great city rushing headlong to its ruin by indulging in an orgy of atrocities perpetrated in the name of " loyalty and civil and religious liberty " upon its Catholic minority, and connived at and encouraged by those in high places, it is refreshing to have to record the courageous protest made at the City Council by a Protestant Unionist member, Mr. Thomas Alexander, solicitor. Denouncing the vendetta, which is ruining the city, he said :

"Much of it could have been avoided. If the spirit of toleration had been shown, Belfast would have been saved the scenes which have gone out to disgrace it in the eyes of the civilised world. The workers would soon find out that they had been fooled."

How unpalatable these biting truths were to the Orange bigots of the City Council can be judged from the astounding proposal of Alderman Duff, a Unionist, that the Press should be asked not to report his colleague's remarks. Some of the Orange Press acted upon this suggestion and suppressed much of Councillor Alexander's speech.

FAILURE OF PACT.

FROM the preceding pages it can be seen how the Collins-Craig Pact was brought to nought. Mr.

Collins honoured his signature immediately by removing the boycott. On the other hand no serious attempt seems to have been made to make the Pact effective in Belfast. Sir James Craig may have intended to fulfil his obligations, but probably found himself helpless before the threats and the operations of the shipyard dictators. He had on previous occasions surrendered himself so compliantly into their power that they were now not in the least disposed to allow him to recover his freedom of action. At any rate, he failed to make good his promise. Under the leadership of the Tregennas, Cootes and "McGuffins of the crowd," the "fight for Protestantism" had to go on ; and the "fight for Protestantism" is a Belfast euphemism for the "extermination of the Papists, Popes, Priests, Holy Water and Holy Marys."

MARCH, 1922

CRESCENDO OF OUTRAGE.

THE task of torpedoing the Collins-Craig Pact, begun immediately after its signing and carried on methodically during the month of February, was continued and intensified during the month of March. The work begun of "evacuating" the Catholic ex-service men recovering from their wounds in two military hospitals was followed up, on March 1, by a murderous attack upon a number of Catholics engaged in relaying the tram-track on the

Antrim Road, a supposed respectable Protestant residential quarter. These Catholic workmen were also ex-soldiers of the British Army who had seen service on many fronts during the European War. Their attackers had probably, many of them, never been in the army, having been among the stay-at-homes who had earned bloated wages on Government work, and who, feeling secure in their indispensability, had clamoured for the application of Conscription knowing that it would not affect themselves. Policemen who endeavoured to arrest these Orange gunmen were frustrated by the intervention of a crowd that had quickly assembled. The miscreants, as usual, were not made amenable.

SAMPLES.

DURING the next two weeks a crescendo of murder, bombing, rioting and general anarchy continued, reaching a maximum towards the middle of the month. Between the 26th of February and the 13th of March the casualties were :

Killed	...	...	27
Wounded	...	...	... 165

Some of the more dastardly of the outrages, of which these casualties were the result, are worthy of brief mention.

On March 4th Owen Hughes, a Catholic from Skegoniel Street, was brutally murdered on the top of a tram by Orange gunmen.

Three Catholic children were seriously wounded

by a bomb thrown into the house of a Catholic, John Press, in Lanark Street.

On March 9th two Catholic funerals were sniped at despite the presence of British armoured cars.

On March 10th Lieutenant Bruce, of the Seaforth Highlanders, who had on several occasions taken measures of protection in favour of Catholics among whom he was, therefore, popular, was murdered just after Curfew. He had been seeing to her home a Catholic young lady to whom he had confided that he was afraid of injury from no one but the Specials.

During the week-end 11—12th, there were seven killed and eight wounded. The smallness of the number of wounded relative to that of the killed indicates the ever-increasing sense of security felt by the Orange murder-gangs in carrying out their operations.

A SNIPER'S FUNERAL.

A NOTORIOUS Orange sniper, H. Hazzard, was shot by the military. His funeral cortège was purposely made to pass through the small Catholic village of Greencastle. The " mourners " indulged in a regular orgy of provocation and atrocities during their passage through the village, shot dead a man named McNally and wrecked and looted many houses. The Orange newspapers thereupon circulated the stereotyped lie that this funeral had been fired at.

GHOULISH DEED.

ON March 12th three armed ruffians knocked at
the door of 99 Great George's Street. Mrs.
Neeson, who was on the eve of her confinement,
opened the door, and as she did so she was shot and
died within a few minutes. Needless to say, she
was a Catholic. Exactly a week before, a bomb had
been thrown into this same house and shop, owned
by William Dempter, a Catholic grocer, and much
damage done to the premises.

A BRILLIANT RUSE!

ON March 13th, by means of a ruse of the Orange
mob, a ghastly atrocity was committed. A false
alarm was given to the fire brigade to come to the
Catholic end of Foundry Street. On their arrival,
a crowd naturally gathered around to see what was
the matter. Thereupon a bomb was hurled into
the middle of the crowd. Twelve were seriously
wounded and awful scenes of agony were witnessed.

CRY FOR MARTIAL LAW.

AT this period there was talk of the imposition of
Martial Law. Such a step would have been
welcomed by the Catholics if its administration were
left entirely in the hands of the military without
any interference from bigoted officials of the Orange
Government. The Coroner, Dr. Graham, at an
inquest said he would like to know how many men
the Lord Mayor wanted murdered before Martial

Law would be brought in. Frequent comment was being made by sensible people on all hands as to why the Lord Mayor was persistently refusing to summon a meeting of city magistrates with a view to devising some means of restoring order to the city.

CRAIG'S OPPOSITION.

THE mystery surrounding this masterly inactivity of the city's chief magistrate was to be revealed later, on the authority of Sir James Craig. On March 14th the latter delivered himself of the following remarks in the Northern Parliament:

" I myself am dead against any suggestion of martial law. . . . . If we have martial law our cause in England will suffer immediately and intensely. They will say one side is as bad as the other."

Could any words more clearly reveal the mentality of the Belfast Government, which is that of a sectarian political party, ever on the *qui-vive* to score a point, to down its political opponents by any means, to whitewash its own enormities, totally indifferent to the universal conception of the functions of government? What does it matter to Sir James Craig if the Catholics are tortured, murdered, sniped, bombed, evacuated and exterminated, without distinction of age, sex or condition, in comparison with such an awful calamity as that " our cause in England will suffer immediately and intensely ?"

What is to be thought of the arrant hypocrisy of the man who, in view of all that has happened in Belfast, still seeks to have the world believe that his criminal followers are not as bad as their victims !

LORD LONDONDERRY LETS SLIP A WORD.

As to the danger of the English people saying that "one side is as bad as the other," we quote the following extract from the speech on the same occasion of Sir James Craig's Cabinet colleague, Lord Londonderry :

> "The fact that a section of those who saw eye to eye with them (*i.e.* with the Belfast Government) on the political situation were implicated in outrages as reprehensible as those committed by Sinn Fein was placing their Government in an impossible situation. When negotiating with British Ministers, he should like to appear before them with clean hands. That was by no means the case now."

These words are remarkable as being the first admission, tentative it is true, of any conduct on the part of the Orange population not altogether consistent with angelic virtue.   Tentative, however, as this admission is, it is in strong contrast to the blatant perversity and hypocrisy of Sir James Craig's reasons against the imposition of Martial Law—reasons which, after twenty months of effort by the Orange side to drive out the Catholics by boycotting, burning, bombing, shooting, looting and murdering, were not very complimentary to British intelligence.

CATHOLICS BURY PROTESTANT VICTIM.

WE have pleasure in recording one incident which relieves the sordid gloom of this tragic period. Herbert Woods, a Protestant victim of the riots, was buried on March 13th by Catholics, who accompanied his remains in immense numbers to the gates of the Protestant Cemetery. Rev. Mr. Dunlop, who officiated at the grave, referred to the tolerant action of the Catholics. He had come all the way, he said, through the Catholic district of the Falls, but he did not need any protection, for he knew that the Catholics would not harm him no matter where he went.

SUPPRESSION.

THESE remarks shared the same fate at the hands of the Orange Press as did those of Councillor Alexander referred to before. They were suppressed. The truth of Mr. Dunlop's statement is borne out by the significant fact that a number of Protestant Churches in the Catholic area of the Falls have never, even in the wildest days of disorder and passion, been interfered with,*nor have their congregations or ministers been ever molested.

The second half of March is just a continuance of the conditions of the first half, culminating on the 24th in what has come to be known as the

_*See exceptional incident, page 134.

McMahon Massacre. From the 15th to the 24th the casualties were :

Killed	...	...	...	23
Wounded	...	...	...	40

Amongst the killed were William Kane, a Catholic milk vendor, pursued into a shop in Newtownards Road and shot dead by an Orange gang. Another brutal murder was that of a Catholic young man, Augustus Orange, shot dead on the morning of the 18th, when returning home after Curfew from a Patrick's Night Ceilidh in St. Mary's Hall. James Hillis, a Catholic, died in hospital on March 20th. He was shot, then brutally beaten, his head battered in and his teeth kicked out. Of the twenty-three killed, the large majority were Catholics, and the same is true of the wounded.

During this period six bomb outrages occurred, all against Catholics. A bomb was hurled into the playground of St. Matthew's Catholic School during play hour. Fortunately the children had not been allowed out that day. Another bomb was flung into the porch of St. Matthew's Church, wounding two women, Madge Carson, 25, Sheriff Street, and Rose Martin, 13, Arnon Street.

THE McMAHON MASSACRE.

ON March 24th occurred the McMahon massacre. This horror received such publicity at the time that only its main outlines need be touched upon here. At 1.20 a.m. five men dressed partially in uniform burst in the door of 3 Kennaird Terrace, Antrim Road, the residence of a well-known business man, Mr. McMahon. The members of the family were aroused and the male members, including the father, his five sons and a shopman, Edward McKenney, were driven into the sitting-room. Here they were ranged against the wall and shot. Three of the sons and the shopman were killed outright. Two other sons and the father were seriously wounded, the latter dying a few hours later in hospital. This tragedy was alleged to be a reprisal for the shooting of two policemen on the previous day.

ARNON STREET BUTCHERY.

THE assassination of the McMahon family fairly shocked a great portion of the civilised world. It was to be followed just one week after by a butchery in several respects even more revolting. This was known as *The Arnon Street Massacre,* in which half-a-dozen people were slaughtered *by police* in the dead of night. The following from the June number of *Studies,* a high-class quarterly, by a painstaking investigator* who visited the scenes described, is worth quoting :

" Stanhope Street stands high and looks down across a boundary street, held by soldiers as I passed, into the Old Lodge Road, leading towards the heart of the city. The latter is an Orange street that bends after about 200 yards and is then lost to view.

* Rev. P. J. Gannon, S.J.

E

It was here that at 10.30 p.m. on April 1 Constable Turner was shot dead by a rifle bullet. Who fired it? The Catholic Committee of Defence in a telegram to Mr. Churchill denied that any Catholic did so. The people of the district say they certainly were not responsible for it. I was even told, though I give it with reserve, that at a military inquiry the soldiers said it could not have come from Stanhope Street.''

INQUIRY REFUSED.

" As Sir J. Craig obstinately refused the inquiry pressed for, both by the Catholic Committee and Mr. Collins, we must leave it at that. Word was soon brought to Brown Square Barracks, and before 11.30 some lorries of R.I.C. and Specials came along. The police got down and started raiding at No. 15 Stanhope Street. Bursting in the door, they cried out, 'Where are the men?' Two were living in this house, but when the lorries were heard in the street, one of them, Joseph McRory, ran out by the back door and into the yard of the next house. But other police were already there and he came back to the yard of No. 15.

" Meantime the other man, whom we shall call H. (as he still lives, his name had better not be given), thought of his two children, and, rushing upstairs, took one under each arm, seizing also an old quilt. He then hurried out to the little yard, where he lay down among a mass of *debris*, placed his children beside him and drew the quilt over all three. I saw the spot and was filled with astonishment that, even in the dark, the ruse could have succeeded in such a space.

" McRory would seem to have lost his head or his nerve. H. begged him to fly, but he said, 'I can't; we're surrounded.' Meantime the saviours of Belfast had broken through the doors. One covered McRory with a revolver and shouted, 'Hands up!' McRory put up his hands, exclaiming, 'Oh, son, I never harmed anyone. 'None of your " sonning " me,' was the reply. A few shots rang out and

Joseph McRory, a middle-aged man of peaceful dis-
position, fell dead.

"No men apparently were found in the other
houses until No. 26, Park Street, off Stanhope Street,
was reached.   Here they came upon a sailor, just
home from sea, named Bernard McKenna.   Rushing
up to the bedroom, where he was standing near the
fire, half-undressed, they shot him several times. He
leaves seven children.

"The next house where a victim was unearthed
was 16, Arnon Street, parallel to Stanhope Street.
In this William Spallin dwelt, who that very day had
buried his wife, herself the victim of some earlier affray.
He was in bed with his grandchild, a boy of twelve
years.   The little lad is said to have shouted: ' Kill
me; dont kill daddy,' as he called his grandfather.
But they shot the old man—aged seventy. Half-an-
hour later the child was found still sitting up in the
bed gazing in horror at the murdered man and
exclaiming: ' Look at daddy! Look at daddy!'

POLICEMAN USES SLEDGE-HAMMER TO MURDER EX-SOLDIER.

"No. 18 Arnon Street was next visited, and here
the climax was reached.   Even to see the scene and
hear the story a fortnight later caused a sense of
nausea.   A family named Walsh lived in the house,
of whom the two adult men—brothers—were ex-
soldiers who had been through the Great War. As
the policemen were beating with a sledge-hammer at
the door, the old mother thought it best to open it.
They then swept past her and up the narrow stairs
to the bedroom where Joseph Walsh lay, with his son
Michael (aged seven) on one side and little Brigid
(aged two) on the other.   They fired some shots,
for three were found in Michael, who died next morning.   Whether they shot the father or not no one
seemed to know.   But the sledge-hammer sufficed.
The priest who came to the house within half-an-hour
told me what he saw. *The skull was open and empty;*
while the whole mass of the brains was on the bolster
almost a foot away.   On descending they found a

young lad, Frank Walsh, aged fourteen, crouching
in the kitchen.   Him they kicked and shot in the
thigh, but not fatally.   Thus was Constable Turner
avenged.

"I asked to see the room upstairs.   The wife
shrank from conducting me.   She had not ventured
to enter it since that night.   But the brother, an ex-
soldier, had stronger nerves and showed me all—the
bolster soaked with blood, and the two straw mat-
tresses deeply stained with it.   He even raised them
up and pointed out pieces of the skull upon the floor,
and fragments of dried brain.   How they swung a
sledge-hammer in that narrow space I know not.
But the blow smashed the skull as it would a cocoa-
nut.   The brother presented me with a few small
pieces in paper, and I still retain this gruesome trophy
of Belfast civilisation and an empire's gratitude to
the men who fought for it.

"'And, Father,' said the brother, 'poor Joseph
was all over the Holy Land and used to tell us all
about the holy places.'

"The Northern Premier has been repeatedly
pressed to grant an impartial inquiry into events of
that night, but has always declined.   The precisest
information has been laid before him implicating his
own police.   Yet no pressure can obtain the slightest
attempt to bring the culprits to justice."

APRIL, 1922

A FAIRY GODMOTHER.

IT is a political platitude that an unjust and perse-
cuting Government is in most cases a very expensive
luxury for a community.   Yet the Belfast Government, whose financial straits have already often been
dilated upon by its own Ministers, has never found
any necessity to use a "Geddes' Axe" to cut down

expenditure on the machinery devised for the per-
secution, expropriation, and extermination of the
Catholic minority.   In this matter the Belfast
Government have at their beck and call a Fairy
Godmother whose prodigality has oftentimes of
late been the subject of grateful comment by Sir
James Craig.   The Fairy Godmother is the
British Government.   Speaking in the House of
Commons on the 27th March, Mr. Churchill said :

" We have placed very large military forces in
Ulster and we will place larger ones if they are
needed.   We have issued over 15,000 rifles and a
considerable proportion of transport to the Ulster
Special Police, and we are bearing out of monies pro-
vided by this House very heavy expenditure for the
maintenance of the police, of whom 25,000, armed
and unarmed, are at present mobilised."[*]

A few weeks later the number of " Specials "
was officially placed at 49,000.

PACT No. 2.

On the 30th March a second and comprehensive
Pact was signed in London between representatives
of the Provisional Government and of the Northern
Government and countersigned on behalf of the
British Government.   The text is as follows :

[*] Included in a Supplementary Estimate for the British Civil
Service issued on the 20th July, 1922, is an item of £2,225.000 for
a grant in aid of the Six County Area as a contribution towards
Present abnormal expenditure, "not to be audited in detail," and
balance, *if any*, to be returned.

IRELAND.

HEADS OF AGREEMENT BETWEEN THE PROVISIONAL GOVERNMENT AND GOVERNMENT OF NORTHERN IRELAND:

I. Peace is to-day declared.

II. From to-day the two Governments undertake to co-operate in every way in their power with a view to the restoration of peaceful conditions in the unsettled areas.

III. The police in Belfast to be organised in general in accordance with the following conditions:

    (1) Special police in mixed districts to be composed half of Catholics and half of Protestants, special arrangements to be made where Catholics or Protestants are living in other districts. All Specials not required for this force to be withdrawn to their homes and their arms handed in.

    (2) An Advisory Committee, composed of Catholics, to be set up to assist in the selection of Catholic recruits for the Special Police.

    (3) All police on duty, except the usual secret service, to be in uniform and officially numbered.

    (4) All arms and ammunition issued to police to be deposited in barracks in charge of a military or other competent officer when the policeman is not on duty, and an official record to be kept of all arms issued, and of all ammunition issued and used.

    (5) Any search for arms to be carried out by police forces composed half of Catholics and half of Protestants, the military rendering any necessary assistance.

IV. A Court to be constituted for the trial without jury of persons charged with serious crime, the Court to consist of the Lord Chief Justice and one of the Lords Justices of Appeal of Northern Ireland. Any person committed for trial for a serious crime to be tried by that Court—

(a) if he so requests, or

(b) if the Attorney-General for Northern Ireland so directs.

Serious crime should be taken to mean any offence punishable with death, penal servitude, or imprisonment for a term exceeding six months. The Government of Northern Ireland will take steps for passing the legislation necessary to give effect to this Article.

V. A Committee to be set up in Belfast of equal numbers, Catholic and Protestant, with an independent Chairman, preferably Catholic and Protestant alternately in successive weeks, to hear and investigate complaints as to intimidation, outrages, etc., such Committee to have direct access to the heads of the Government. The local Press to be approached with a view to inserting only such reports 'of disturbances, etc., as shall have been considered and communicated by this Committee.

VI. I.R.A. activity to cease in the Six Counties, and thereupon the method of organising the Special Police in the Six Counties outside Belfast shall proceed as speedily as possible upon lines similar to those agreed to for Belfast.

VII. During the month immediately following the passing into law of the Bill confirming the Constitution of the Free State (being the month within which the Northern Parliament is to exercise its option) and before any address in accordance with Article 12 of the Treaty is presented, there shall be a further meeting between the signatories to this agreement with a view to ascertaining:

(a) whether means can be devised to secure the unity of Ireland.

(b) Failing this, whether agreement can be arrived at on the boundary question otherwise than by recourse to the Boundary

Commission outlined in Article 12 of the Treaty.

VIII. The return to their homes of persons who have been expelled to be secured by the respective Governments, the advice of the Committee mentioned in Article 5 to be sought in cases of difficulty.

IX. In view of the special conditions consequent on the political situation in Belfast and neighbourhood, the British Government will submit to Parliament a vote not exceeding £500,000 for the Ministry of Labour of Northern Ireland to be expended exclusively on relief work, one-third for the benefit of Roman Catholics and two-thirds for the benefit of Protestants. The Northern signatories agree to use every effort to secure the restoration of the expelled workers, and wherever this proves impracticable at the moment, owing to trade depression, they will be afforded employment on the relief works referred to in this Article so far as the one-third limit will allow, Protestant ex-service men to be given first preference in respect to the two-thirds of the said fund.

X. The two Governments shall, in cases agreed upon between the signatories, arrange for the release of political prisoners in prison for offences before the date hereof. No offences committed after March 31st, 1922, shall be open to consideration.

XI. The two Governments unite in appealing to all concerned to refrain from inflammatory speeches and to exercise restraint in the interests of peace.

Signed on behalf of the PROVISIONAL GOVERNMENT:

> MICHAL O COILEAIN,
> E. S. O DUGGAIN,
> CAOIMHGIN O HUIGIN,
> ART O GRIOBHTHA.

Signed on behalf of the GOVERNMENT OF NORTHERN IRELAND:

JAMES CRAIG
LONDONDERRY,
E. M. ARCHDALE.

Countersigned on behalf of the BRITISH GOVERN-MENT:

WINSTON S. CHURCHILL,
L. WORTHINGTON EVANS,
HAMAR GREENWOOD.

THE QUESTION—PEACE OR WAR?

ONCE again are we in presence of the struggle for mastery between the '' Will to Peace '' and the '' Will to War.'' On the one side we have the Northern Government through its signatories becoming a party to an agreement of which the very first term is '' Peace is to-day declared '' and of which the remaining terms, if carried out in earnest, gave considerable promise of restoring some semblance of civilization to Belfast. But on the other hand, stands the army of Specials whose existence as a '' Pretorian Guard '' of the Ulster junker was threatened by the very terms of the Pact, and in the background stand the mob, the Orange lodges, the '' boys,'' the murder gangs, whilst decent Protestants are cowed into silence by the gunmen. What is the issue going to be? Is the new Pact to meet the same fate as the former one?

THE ANSWER.

THE issue was not left long in doubt. After signing the first Collins-Craig Agreement in February, a short lull supervened. But it was only a lull. Full activities were afoot again. But this time there was not even a lull. The Pact was issued from the Colonial Office, London, on the night of the 30th March. It appeared in the Press of the 31st March. On the night of the 1st April, within forty-eight hours of its issue, was perpetrated the most horrible as yet of the Belfast massacres, known as Arnon Street butchery, described above, in which half-a-dozen people were slaughtered *by police* in dead of night.

WHO RULES IN BELFAST?

THE Arnon Street massacre was the answer prompt and decisive of the " boys " and the Specials to the politicians, or, as Mr. Tregenna on a former occasion styled them, " the intriguers in the Belfast Parliament," who may have foolishly thought that the bestowal of peace was within their power. But, as on a previous occasion, the Belfast Government were quickly brought up against the realities of the situation. They were only a Government in name and would be allowed to govern just in so far as their armed forces and mobs would allow. No wonder that at a later date Sir James Craig, when trying to explain away his failure to honour the Pact, was compelled feebly to admit that certain occurrences rendered the carrying out of its terms impossible. In fact, so completely had the intransigeant elements gained the upper hand that when the Advisory Committee mentioned in the Pact was got together the Specials actually arrested some of the Catholic members and attempted to arrest the remainder.

The month of April keeps fairly up to its ghastly opening in its record of tragedies. In addition to those slaughtered on the night of the Arnon Street massacre there were 31 violent deaths during the month. Of these the majority were Catholics. One was Bernard McMahon, the fifth victim of the McMahon massacre. Another was Michael Walsh, aged seven, who died as a result of wounds received in the Arnon Street massacre. A third was Mary Owens who died of the effects of the bomb thrown amongst the crowd of children at play in Weaver Street on 13th February.

FIELD DAYS.

SOME days a bloodier toll was exacted than on others. For instance, on the 14th at least four murders were committed. Three of them seem to have been clearly the work of the same Orange gang, and the singular thing is that two of the victims were Protestants who, owing to the circumstances, were undoubtedly mistaken for Catholics.

In quite a number of instances during the past two years it has been only too clear that such tragic mistakes were made. The same day a Catholic locomotive man at the Midland Railway was shot dead while cleaning his engine.

RED RUIN.

ON the 17th the little Catholic quarter of Marrowbone was assailed by a furious Orange horde returning from a football match, as on several previous occasions. The unfortunate residents were terrorised by revolver firing for hours, several of them were wounded and then the attackers wound up the business by wholesale looting and burning of houses. Fifty Catholic families had to fly from their blazing homesteads. Antigua Street was practically burned out, Saunderson Street fared little better. The fire-bugs did their work leisurely and thoroughly, and did it under the eyes of large numbers of British Crown forces and Special Police paid by British money. These, (if they did not actually assist the incendiary mob, and it has been widely alleged that they did), made no serious effort to prevent the destruction. Whatever little property those poor people had was for the most part looted by their "loyalist" neighbours before the houses were fired. What could not be carried away was smashed or burned. Three were killed and seventeen seriously injured in connection with this orgy.

WOMEN AND BABIES.

ON the 19th five more Catholics were slaughtered. Two of them were young women, Mrs. Donegan and Miss Berry. They were pursued upstairs by a gang and deliberately shot dead. Another was a child of thirteen, Mary Keenan, shot fatally as she was playing at a lamp-post, whilst her baby companion was wounded also. A fourth was Patrick McGoldrick, butchered in his own shop.

On the 21st five more victims are registered— four Catholics and one Protestant, murdered apparently as a reprisal. On the 22nd a Protestant lad of seventeen, named Best, who had been frequently seen attending a Catholic hospital to get his hand treated, was found shot dead in an exclusively Protestant area. Another mistake, clearly enough.

ST. MATTHEW'S CHURCH AGAIN.

ON the evening of the 23rd (Sunday), as the people were going into their church in Ballymacarrett for devotions, a bomb was hurled into the door of the sacred edifice from the Orange street adjacent, Bryson Street. A most respectable woman, Mrs. McCabe, was killed, a policeman and some others wounded. This is at least the sixth bomb hurled at the same church. An " official " version of this incident was published by the Belfast Government which would do credit to Sir Hamar Greenwood himself

AND A PROTESTANT CHURCH.

ON April 9th a number of Catholic youngsters, none of whom was over fifteen years of age, got into Albert Street Presbyterian Church and did some damage, carrying off part of the communion plate. The young miscreants were rounded up by their parents and several of the Catholic neighbours and the purloined property was, as far as possible, restored. The nasty outrage was strongly condemned.

From a most reliable source we take the following summary of atrocities committed on Catholics from the 1st of the month until this date, 24th :

Murdered, 14 men, 3 women and 4 children.
Attempted murders, 27.
Wounded, 39.
Houses looted and burned, 75.
Houses bombed, 5.
Families evicted, 89.
Persons homeless, 357.

From the agonies suffered by many people during this terrible time, one instance, not the only one of its kind, may be recorded.

On the 18th April Mrs. McKnight, of 58, Glenview Street, mother of nine children, confined at 6.30 a.m., was driven from her home by an Orange mob at noon the same day.

AN ASTOUNDING MANIFESTO.

HERE a reference may be made to a document signed and issued by the heads of the Protestant

churches in Belfast, by way of rejoinder to a pro-
test made by the Catholic hierarchy against the
denial to Catholics in Belfast of the natural right
to earn their daily bread, etc. The signatories are
Dr. D'Arcy, Protestant Archbishop of Armagh ;
Dr. Grierson, Protestant Bishop of Down and
Connor and Dromore ; Dr. Lowe, Moderator of the
Presbyterian General Assembly ; and Rev. W. H.
Smyth, President of the Methodist Conference.

The statements made therein are amazing in
view of the widely known and acknowledged facts.
We must only assume that the right rev. and rev.
signatories have not gone beyond the discredited
Orange Press for their information on the subject
in hand :

" It is not true," they say, " that Roman Catholics
have been denied their natural right to earn their
daily bread. The shipyard workers did not exclude
any man because of his religion. A reign of terror
was organized by gangs of gunmen, who encamped
in certain quarters of the city of Belfast, made war
upon its people, throwing bombs into tramcars full of
workers, and savagely shooting down men, women
and children. This was an attempt to intimidate the
loyalists. It is not true that able-bodied Protestants
are supplied with arms to harass their Roman
Catholic neighbours. The Northern Government is
showing itself quite impartial in its efforts to put
down all illegal use and carrying of arms. The fact
is that the trouble in Belfast is political and not
religious. It is an effort to paralyse the Northern
Government. Speaking for the clergy and people of
the churches we represent, we can conscientiously
affirm that we and our people are, and have been,
doing everything in our power to prevent the struggle

from becoming a religious one. We deeply regret the
fact that there have been reprisals. It is not an easy
thing for a powerful majority to submit tamely to
such treatment at the hands of an aggressive
minority. But we have done everything in our power
to prevent the dreadful competition in evil which is
the inevitable consequence of reprisals. Special services and public meetings have been held for the
express purpose of denouncing murder, by whomsoever committed, and of warning against rendering
evil for evil. As to the Northern Government, it has
shown in many ways its earnest desire that Roman
Catholics should have their full share in the public
and private life of Northern Ireland. It has offered
them many appointments. It is ready to give them
more than their share in its police forces. It is
eagerly anxious that they should claim and enjoy
equal rights with all others in the citizenship of
Northern Ireland.''

It is hoped that the present volume, though
giving but a mere fraction of the two years' outrages on Belfast Catholics, will be found a sufficient
reply to the statements, unsupported by evidence
of any kind, issued by the four heads of the
Protestant churches.

A SAMPLE!

IT will be sufficient to point out here that the first
definitely traceable act of aggression alleged by the
learned signatories as a reason for excluding
thousands of Catholics from their work in July,
1920, was a bomb thrown at a tramcar full of
pogromist workmen on 22nd November, 1921—
just sixteen months after. The first bomb thrown

in Belfast by either side in connection with the pogrom was a year after the expulsions from the shipyards, 11th June, 1921 ; *and that and four-teen other bomb outrages were perpetrated upon Catholics by Orange ruffians before a Catholic was even accused of throwing a bomb.**

Following is a list of the pogrom bombings for 1921 :

June 11.—Two bombs in Dock Lane. One killed, others wounded.

July 14.—Bomb exploded in house of Mary Leonard, 7, Garmoyle Street.

August 21.—Tyrone Street. Six injured.

August 22.—North Queen Street. (Didn't explode).

August 27·—House of Mr. Moan wrecked.

August 29.—Several bombs in Vere Street area. No damage.

September 2.—Mrs. Doherty's, Boundary Street. Woman injured.

September 19.—Little Patrick Street. Two dud bombs.

September 20.—Glenview Street. Two men wounded.

September 21.—House in Beechfield Street.

September 23.—Into Foundry Street. Woman injured.

September 25.—Bomb thrown into Seaforde Street. Thrown back. Two killed and thirty-four wounded.

September 26.—Bomb thrown among children in Milewater Street. Ex-soldier killed, several children wounded.

* A Catholic was, indeed, accused, and, as is well known, wrongly accused, and was sentenced to penal servitude for a bomb thrown at the military in April. This, however, had nothing at all to do with the pogrom.

October 16.—Bomb thrown into Seaforde Street.

November 14.—Bomb thrown into Catholic quarter in Ballymacarrett; bursts in air.

November 22.—Tramcar bombed in Corporation Street. Two killed, several injured.

November 24.—Tramcar bombed in Royal Avenue. One killed, sixteen wounded.

November 29.—Bomb thrown into Keegan Street (Catholic). Kills Mrs. McNamara, mother of eight.

December 28.—Bomb thrown into Falls Road.

Fourteen out of the first fifteen cases above mentioned have never been for a moment in doubt. The bombs were all, without exception, hurled into Catholic houses or Catholic streets. The only instance where question might have been raised was that of the bomb thrown back from Seaforde Street, September 25th.

MAY, 1922

WORST MONTH OF ALL.

THE last week of April and the first week of May, though far from peaceful, witnessed a welcome improvement in the Belfast situation. On the 10th and 11th the Orange terrorism began to break forth again by frequent firing into the Catholic districts of Ardoyne and the Marrowbone.

On the 12th a brutal murder occurred in the former area. Michael Cullen, a quiet Catholic man of middle age, residing at 27, Havanna

Street, was held up on his way home from
work by a murder gang of four who made him hold
up his hands, demanding whether he was a
Catholic; and on his replying, " What is that to
you?" fired several shots into him. These
particulars were ascertained from the victim himself in the Mater Hospital before his death a little
later.

AN ORANGE FUNERAL.

ON the 13th and 14th four more lives were taken,
including a little girl (Catholic) of thirteen shot
dead by a sniper in Marine Street. A dozen were
wounded. One of the men killed was an Orangeman named Beattie, and on the occasion of his
funeral on the 16th large numbers of the
" mourners " behaved in a most riotous and revolting way, not quite uncommon at Orange funerals
for some time past. Large gangs of them swept
along in front of the remains, ordered people on
every side, if they thought they were Catholics,
and always in a gross, offensive manner, to un-
cover, even while the hearse was still perches
away. People who did not do so promptly enough
were in many instances mauled. Hats of by-
standers were knocked off. The hooligan
" mourners " also rushed into Catholic houses
along the route compelling the owners to lower the
blinds, and conducting themselves with great
insolence meanwhile. Some shots were fired in

the neighbourhood, and then an armoured car fired into a small Catholic street. Who fired the first shots may be hard to ascertain, but those familiar with Belfast Orange methods will not readily believe that they were fired by Catholics. Nobody at the funeral was hit, of course, and the military got an excuse for firing into a Catholic street. That is how the game is commonly played by the Orangemen.

Farther on along the route someone *was* hit. At the door of a fruit shop in North Street, a Catholic young man of twenty-one, named Madden, was busy unloading cases from his van when about twenty of those "mourners," leaving the funeral procession in Royal Avenue, walked up to the youth and one of them said, "What religion are you—are you a Catholic?" Madden smiled, but made no reply. Then the ruffian drew a revolver and shot him through the heart.

Another Catholic was killed next day; five the day following.

On the 19th three Protestant men were killed while at work in Little Patrick Street. A constable (Protestant) pursuing some men engaged in a hold-up was fatally shot in Millfield.

TWELVE PLUS ONE.

ON the 20th the murder gangs operated over several areas of the city and thirteen persons were slain, twelve Catholics and one Protestant and nearly a score were wounded. A Catholic lady and her daughter, Mrs. and Miss Shiels, were shot, though not fatally, by a gang who invaded their house in Alexandra Park Avenue. The congregation were fired upon when leaving St. Matthew's Catholic Church, one man being shot through the body. The small Catholic group in Weaver Street area were attacked in great force and most of them driven out at the point of the revolver, one resident being killed during the operations.

On the 21st (Sunday) a Catholic young man, Hugh MacDonald, was dragged from a tram in an Orange quarter and *kicked to death* on the street. His head and face were in pulp on his arrival at the hospital.

On the 22nd three Catholics and three Protestants were done to death, one of the latter being Mr. W. J. Twaddell, a Member of the Northern Parliament.

Two died from wounds on the 23rd. Three were slain on the 24th. Five, including a girl of nineteen (Catholic), were murdered, and one died of wounds on the 25th. On each of these days large numbers were wounded.

BEATEN AND THEN DROWNED.

AMONG the victims of the 25th was Jack O'Hare, a porter well known in one of the city hotels. He was a Catholic. Going home across the Albert Bridge about 10 o'clock he was surrounded by an Orange gang who knocked him down and kicked him till they thought he was dead. They were on the point of leaving him to look for further victims, no doubt, when he managed to ask for a drink. The loyalists thereupon turned back and again attacked him. They lifted and flung him over the parapet of the bridge into the river beneath, where he cried once or twice for help and then sank to his death. Special police and military were standing only a few yards from where this horror was perpetrated. His friends when dragging the river for his body on the six following days were frequently fired upon.

Two were killed on the 26th. One of these, Alexander Morrison, was a Protestant from Ballyclare, murdered, obviously by being mistaken for a Catholic, in an exclusively loyalist district on Albert Bridge Road.

The 27th had three dead, and the 29th three more, with a big batch of wounded each day.

FRIGHTFULNESS.

BUT the 31st of May will always be remembered as probably the most hideous date in the two years of horrors in Belfast.

Two men, shortly after four o'clock, came up to two Special Constables standing at the corner of a street in Millfield and, drawing revolvers, shot one of them fatally and wounded the other. There are very few Catholics in Belfast who would not strongly condemn a murderous act of this kind.

Who the perpetrators were probably none but themselves know.   It is morally certain that none of
the people of Millfield had the slightest knowledge
of, or connection, or sympathy with the authors of
the deed.

Yet large numbers of the Special Constabulary
immediately rushed into the district and from
armoured cars and Lancia cars poured indiscriminate fire of machine guns and rifles among the
unarmed and inoffensive people on all sides for
well on a couple of hours.   Of course all who could
find shelter quickly did so.

At the first outburst a horse and van, coming
directly in the line of machine gun fire, was probably the means of saving several lives as the street
beyond was fairly crowded, especially with children,
at the time.   The horse fell dead, riddled with
bullets.   The driver had a marvellous escape.

PRESBYTERY ATTACKED.

THE fire of the Specials was renewed again towards eight or nine o'clock, but the streets in the
Catholic areas were all deserted.   They tried hard,
however, to find victims by firing through windows
and doors.   They broke open the doors of
McEntee's public-house in King Street and,
assisted by their officers, looted practically all the
large stock of drink in the place.   At a late hour,
and in a pretty drunken state, they drew up in front
of St. Mary's Presbytery also in King Street,

where three priests, together with domestics, reside, and fired many volleys into it, smashing all the windows, ripping the inner walls and ceilings, and doing a good deal of other damage. Luckily the inmates succeeded in getting into positions of safety.

BILLY ON THE WARPATH.

MEANWHILE the Orange mobs seized this opportunity of proving their loyalty, and broke loose upon their Catholic neighbours in various parts of the town.

MOTHER AND DAUGHTER MURDERED.

A CROWD of those braves rushed into the house of Mr. McIlroy, butcher, 28 Old Lodge Road, found only Mrs. McIlroy and her daughter there and shot them both dead.

The total number of killed on that day were 11 ; of seriously wounded, 16.

EXTENSIVE BURNING.

FOURTEEN houses were burned out in Peter's Place. In one of these the firemen were shocked to find the dead bodies of a man and a woman. On examination it was discovered that *both of them had been shot before the house was set on fire.*

Boyd Street was invaded by the Orange mob and burned almost from end to end, the unfortunate residents having to fly for their lives.

The number of Catholic families driven out
and rendered homeless on that one day were :

Posnett Street	6
Maryville Street	12
Hardcastle Street	6
Woodford Street	14
Lower Canning Street	3
Lower California Street	12
Peter's Place	14
Norfolk Street	3
Cupar Street	3
Grosvenor Place	2
Grosvenor Road	11

On 19th May 71 families were driven out, chiefly
from Mountcollyer Street and Leopold Street.

On 20th May 148 families were driven out of the
Weaver Street area (where the children were
slaughtered by an Orange bomb, Feb. 13), including Shore Street, Milewater Street, North Derby
Street and Jennymount Street. The people in
this district are of the poorest mill-working class.

No wonder nearly 1000 penniless refugees
reached Glasgow within the next few days.

The special correspondent of the *Manchester
Guardian* refers to

" the eviction from their homes by Orange mobs, led
by Specials, of thousands of defenceless Catholics.
. . . . The combatants in this feud are on the
one hand a handful of Catholic gunmen, which even
Orange opinion estimates at hundreds out of the
93,243 Catholics in Belfast. On the other hand, the
semi-armed Orange mobs drawn from the 293,791
Protestants in Belfast, and the armed Special Constabulary, who are largely recruited from the Orange
mobs, and frequently work in close co-operation with
them. The great bulk of the victims of the feud are

to be found in the 93,000 unarmed defenceless Catholics.

"On these unfortunate beings the fury of Orange Specials, and Orange mob unable to reach the Catholic gunmen, and fortified by sectarian animosity, falls daily and nightly. These people have committed no offence unless it be an offence to be born a Catholic. In politics great numbers of them are Constitutionalist Nationalists. Many thousands are ex-soldiers who served during the War.

"On the simple charge of being Catholics, hundreds of families are being continually driven from their houses. . . . . In these operations the 'Specials' provide the petrol, fire-arms, and immunity from interruption.

"Protestant civilians, too, suffer from this type of warfare, but to a comparatively slight extent, and the Catholics killed and wounded enormously outnumber the Protestants. Casualties among Protestant women and children are rare; amongst Catholics heavy."

JUNE, 1922

BURNING A WOMAN.

THE month of June was ushered in with the setting fire to a woman and the attempt to burn her alive. The facts are still fresh in the public memory, but may be briefly recalled.

Miss Susan McCormack, a Catholic, and housekeeper to a Catholic physician in Donegall Pass, went to answer a ring at 9.15 p.m. and found a gang of men at the door. They said they were looking for the doctor. She told them he was not at home. They rushed into the hall, knocked the woman down, kicked her about the body, head and

face.   They produced a tin of petrol, sprinkled
her clothes and hair with it, applied a match and
then cleared off.   The poor woman ran out scream-
ing, a mass of flame, and some of the neighbours
hurried to her assistance.   She was removed to
hospital in a very critical condition.

For a wonder, the Orange Press yielded so far
as to utter a specific denunciation.

Even the *Belfast Telegraph,* in a strong editorial
reference, said :

" The nature that can violate the primal instinct
of civilisation has sunk to something as low as
savagery.   Even the brutes of the field exhibit a
natural chivalry in this respect, and protect their
females.   The setting alight of the clothes of a
servant yesterday evening was a deed of unqualified
shame, and those who descended to an act so contemptible and cruel should be hunted out of society.
They are not fit to be at large."

AN OMISSION.

SIR JAMES CRAIG did not send the usual message
about " admirable restraint," etc. •

The number of people killed in Belfast in June
was relatively small, being only 19, and the wounded
scarcely 100.   As compared with the 75 killed and
163 wounded in May, this is a great falling off.
The vast majority of the victims were Catholics.

WHOLESALE EVICTIONS.

BUT if June showed a decrease in murder, it showed
a big increase in the number of Catholic families

evicted from their homes. In the first week these reached the staggering total of 436 as compared with 404 Catholic families evicted in the whole month of May.

REFUGEES.

No wonder that Catholic refugees from Belfast have been crowding into Dublin and every other town in Southern Ireland, as well as into Glasgow and other places across the water. Since July, 1920, some 20,000 of them have been driven from their homes in the Protestant areas of Belfast. Many of these were absorbed in some way into the already congested Catholic districts, but a point was reached when further absorption became impossible, and then thousands were obliged to clear out of the infernal city and out of the Six-County area.

SPECIALS ATTACK HOSPITAL.

THE Special Constabulary surpassed themselves when, during Curfew on the night of the 5th June, they attacked the Mater Infirmorum Hospital with rifle and revolver fire which was kept up for three-quarters of an hour, riddling windows, smashing furniture in the wards and paralysing all the patients, as well as the sisters and doctors, with terror. Fortunately none were killed, as everyone was stretched on the floor or in some place of hiding.

Of course the Belfast " Home Office " went through a farce of issuing a report intended to exculpate the Special Constables, but such " official" statements are merely sent out for effect in the British and foreign Press, and they do not deceive anyone in Belfast.

Replying to a message from the Superioress of the hospital; the Secretary of the Red Cross Committee in Geneva wired :

" Ready to take all necessary steps. Be good enough only to indicate to what authority we should address ourselves."

The Superioress replied :

" We thank you for your sympathy. Be good enough only to address yourselves to the Government of Great Britain."

MORE MURDERS.

MEANTIME the criminal gangs were active as usual in many parts of the city. Terrorism to a degree reigned everywhere. Several women, as well as men, were shot at and wounded. A Catholic, Patrick O'Malley, was deliberately murdered at his own door in Stratheden Street on the 6th June. Next day another Catholic, John McMenemy, was similarly murdered in Conway Street. When he fell after being shot, the loyalist mob yelled cheers and obscene expressions.

On June the 12th, Mr. E. D. Devine, managing director of Messrs. Bernard Hughes, Ltd., one of the most amiable and highly-esteemed Catholic

gentlemen in the city, after pluckily disarming one
of a gang who raided the office, was, by another of
the gang, shot dead in the presence of his son and
the clerical staff.　　It is probable, however, that
the assailants were a gang of common thieves.

MAGISTRATE ON SPECIALS.

THE conduct of the Special Constabulary throughout the month towards the Catholic citizens has
been described by one of the city justices of peace
as " terrible and disgusting."　　He has seen them,
he says, take the bits of furniture of the poor people
into the street and burn it ; had known them on
raiding houses to abuse children and women, and
even beat their heads against the walls, swaggering
and constantly threatening to shoot.

" Owing to our system of A., B. and C. Constabulary, there is no reason why every loyalist in
Ulster should not have arms in his hands legally,"
said Sir James Craig in the Belfast Parliament.

In Ulster, of course, a " loyalist " is only
another word for a Protestant.

In pursuance of the London Pact a Conciliation
Committee of Catholics and Protestants was formed
in Belfast.　　Sir James Craig's Government showed
their zeal for carrying out the Pact by *arresting
two Catholic members of the Conciliation Committee and issuing warrants for three others.*　These
highly respectable men are in prison without any
charge having been preferred against them.

INCENDIARISM AND MURDER.

A FEATURE of the last month or two has been the great number of fires in which many business concerns were destroyed. There seems good reason to believe that much of this is due to extreme agents on the Catholic side ; nor is it surprising that men driven to desperation by the Orange pogrom of two years should seek to hit back even in this unjustifiable way.

On June 19th, four men knocked at the door of Miss Kelly, 14, Jocelyn Street. When the lady answered the knock one of them held a revolver up to her and demanded if she was a Catholic. Instead of replying, she slammed the door on the intruders, whereupon the ruffian with the revolver fired through it, wounding her seriously in two places. She collapsed and was taken to hospital.

On the 20th, two poor Catholic carters were murdered in most cold-blooded fashion in loyalist districts of the city ; and the next day an old Catholic man of over seventy named Millar was murdered in his own house in the Orange Woodstock Road district by a gang of four who rushed into the place and riddled him with bullets. On the 23rd an Orange gunman deliberately murdered a Catholic boy of seventeen named Leo Rea who was going to his work.

THE END OF A CHAPTER?

On the 27th June, the Lord Mayor made a

special strong appeal for a ten days' truce. Since
then the condition of the city has improved considerably and there are few who do not devoutly
pray that the improvement may be lasting.

"Better late than never" is, however, about the
best one can say of his lordship's action. There
is surely reason to believe that had he and others of
his colleagues, entrusted with providing for the
peace of the city, put forth an earnest effort at the
outbreak of the pogrom hundreds of lives would
have been spared as a result, thousands of wounded
would have escaped their sufferings, the Catholic
population would not have been harried and partly
exterminated, and the name of Belfast might not
have become a byword the world over. The Lord
Mayor was appealed to early in the trouble to take
certain measures, or even to summon a meeting of
the Corporation to devise means for ending the
pogrom, but he refused to exercise his powers.

CRAIG'S PRISON SHIP.

CATHOLICS, many of them belonging to the most
respectable families, have been arrested in hundreds
by the Orange Government and, without any
charge whatever, thrust into prison, or, what is far
worse, sent on board a wretched wooden ship lying
near Carrickfergus. This floating house of filth
and misery is called by the splendid name of the
Argenta. Probably nothing so vile could be found,

even in Turkey, at the present day. The unfortunate prisoners are huddled together in sections of forty like cattle in a pen. The food is execrable, and has to be eaten off the floor. The lavatory accommodations consist of a few buckets placed openly at the end of the apartment. And so on.

FLOGGING.

THE first piece of legislation passed by the Belfast Government was what is known as the " Flogging Act." How it operates will be understood from the following extracts from a letter of an ex-soldier, James McAlorum, written from prison to his wife after the ordeal.

McAlorum is an ex-service man. He joined the British Army in 1909, and served throughout the Great War from 1914 to 1919. He is a Mons hero. After demobilisation in 1919 he was employed in McCausland's, whose works are situated on Queen's Road, beside Harland and Wolff's shipbuilding yard. He was driven from his work by the Orange mob in July, 1920, during the pogrom. After a period of enforced idleness, he was employed at the tramway reconstruction works on Newtownards Road. Again he and his fellow-Catholics were chased from their work by the Orange mob and savagely assaulted. He was again employed at the tramway reconstruction works on the Antrim Road as a foreman ganger.

When working there one day he and his mates

were again attacked and McAlorum was shot in the thigh. After coming out of hospital he was again employed at the same work. He was accused of being along with three or four others who held up a Protestant man in a public-house and assaulted and robbed him of 5s. On the previous day he met with an accident at his work. A tram rail fell on his arm injuring it to such an extent that he had to get seven stitches in his wrist.

The prosecutor, James Arnold, identified McAlorum as one of the men who assaulted him, but swore that he had never seen him before. This man had been drinking in the public-house and may or may not have been in a condition to identify anyone.

The only Crown witness, Annie Maginnes, swore that she had known McAlorum for five or six years previously. She identified him as the one who struck Arnold. She is Arnold's sister-in-law.

The witnesses for the defence swore that McAlorum was not there at the time of the assault.

The doctor's certificate of the injury to his wrist was produced.

At the first trial the jury disagreed and McAlorum was allowed out on bail.

At the second trial he was convicted and sentenced to three years' penal servitude and fifteen strokes of the cat.

The youth, Edward O'Neill, referred to in the statement, was sentenced to three years' penal

servitude and twenty-five strokes of the birch for
being concerned in an armed hold-up.

Here is McAlorum's letter :

"Dear Wife,—After consideration, I feel absolutely compelled to place before you a truthful
account of the degradation which I was subjected to
in this prison on Thursday night, the 22nd June, by
order of the Northern Parliament.

"On the night in question I had just finished my
supper when four warders entered my cell and took
me to an underground dungeon where the officials had
erected what they call a flogging triangle.

"Gathered in a cluster around this instrument of
torture were the prison doctor, governor, a dozen or
so of prison warders and a number of Special Constabulary, all eager to witness the savagery that was
to be enacted there, and of which myself and a few
other unfortunate prisoners, some of them mere
children in their early 'teens, were to be the victims.

"I was stripped to the skin and the warders tied
me hand and foot to the triangle, and when they had
me secured, the Englishman, who was sent over here
specially to administer torture, commenced the bar-
barity.

"When I had received the fifteen lashes, and while
the officials were bandaging my back, I had a look at
the man who had flogged me and the sweat was
running down his face.

"This man, who was almost six feet in height,
had exerted all his strength and energy in inflicting
this savage operation and left my back in such a
state that a whole piece of my skin could not have
been touched from my waist to my neck with the
point of a needle. One of the victims who was led
to the chamber of torture after I had received my
flogging was a mere boy of seventeen years of age,
named Edward O'Neill, and when they had this boy
stripped and tied up, and when the administerer of
the torture commenced his foul work, the agonising
cry of this child-prisoner pleading to the prison
doctor to intervene and save him from the cruel and

unmerciful punishment could be heard all over the prison. It was the yelling of the boy which was the first warning to the other prisoners located in the prison that some of the prison inmates were being maltreated and they gave vent to their feelings by an outburst of protest, shouting and kicking their cell doors, which could have been heard a great distance from the prison and sent consternation into the hearts of the officials, who, for the moment, thought that the civilian populace had broken into the prison.''

Several savage sentences were imposed at the Belfast Commission in July, 1922, by Lord Justice Andrews for the possession of arms.

Accused.	Offence.	Penal Servitude, Years.	"Cat," Lashes.
G. M'Gorrigle,	Webley and 6 rounds ...	3	—
J. Moore,	loaded revolver	3	10
P. M'Grath,	Webley, 2 rounds ...	3	10
P. Bell,	revolver, 3 rounds	3	10
(An ex-soldier who fought at Salonika)			
Thomas Trainor,	Webley, 53 rounds ...	4	10
A. M'Gibben,	revolver	3	—
P. Cosgrave,	revolver	3	15
J. O'Hara,	bomb, revolver, 10 rounds	3	10
W. Morton,	bomb, revolver, 10 rounds	3	—
H. Hanvey,	revolver, 40 rounds ...	4	25
A. Hanvey,	revolver, 40 rounds ...	3	25
A. Canning,	armed robbery	3	15

		Hard Labour, Months.	
T. Hunter,	revolver, 3 rounds	12	10
T. M'Cullogh,	riot	6	—
R. Daly,	stealing scrap iron	6	—
R. M'Clean,	house breaking	6	—
W. Turnbull,	revolver	12	—
E. Digney,	attempted robbery ...	12	—

THE WHITE CROSS

FRIENDS IN NEED.

SOME weeks after the expulsions from the shipyards in 1920 a Relief Committee was formed in Belfast to look after the pressing needs of the victims, a local fund was generously subscribed to, and administered chiefly through the St. Vincent de Paul Society. It was hoped that local effort could tide over the trouble until normal conditions might be restored. But as time passed it became apparent that the persecution was likely to be prolonged. An appeal was therefore made to the charity of the outside public. This met with a prompt and magnanimous response not only from every quarter of Ireland but from various centres abroad. Glasgow sent many large contributions, Birmingham was notable among the places in England that stood by the Belfast sufferers. In Ireland hardly a town or village failed to send assistance. Dublin showed a fine example. In Cork a committee under the chairmanship of a Protestant clergyman set to work in a very thorough manner and for months forwarded a thousand pounds a week to Belfast until their own city was so hideously burned and devastated.

THE AMERICAN WHITE CROSS.

A YEAR passed and the outlook of the victimised workers was still as gloomy as well could be. Close on £150,000 had been sent to their relief chiefly by their southern fellow-countrymen who were all this time suffering from the horrors perpetrated by the Black and Tans. Then the American White Cross came to the general rescue by its noble work for the Relief of Distress in Ireland. The details of that work—which Ireland will never forget— cannot be given here ; but it may be pointed out that for well over a year that magnificent organisation has been contributing from £5,000 to £7,000 a week to sufferers in Belfast alone, besides giving a grant of several thousands to provide houses for some of those whose homes were burned down.

LIST OF THOSE KILLED

IN BELFAST POGROM

From July, 1920, to June, 1922

Catholics 267 : Protestants 185 : Unascertained 3 : Total 455.

(Total of Wounded over 2,000)

1920

21/7/20.	Cath.	Finnegan, Francis (40), Lower Clonard St.
	Cath.	Noad, Maggie (27), 3 Anderson St.
	Cath.	Devlin, Bernard (18), 39 Alexandra St.
22/7/20.	Cath.	Morgan, Brother Michael, Clonard Monastery.
	Cath.	Downey, John, Roden St.
	Cath.	Giles, Joseph, Kashmir Rd.
	Cath.	Gauran, M. Alexandra, Tralee St.
	Cath.	Robinson, Thomas, 6 Kane St.
	Cath.	McAuley, Albert, Stanfield St.
	Prot.	Godfrey, William, Argyle St.
	Prot.	Dunning, William, Bellvue St.
	Prot.	Stewart, James (18), Clydebank, Frome St.
	Prot.	Conn, James A. (33), 47 James St.
	Cath.	Hennessy, Henry (48), 120 Ardilea St.
23/7/20.	Prot.	Weston, Ann, 24 Welland St. (from wounds during attack on Convent).
	Prot.	McCune, William, 22 Clonallen St.
25/7/20.	Cath.	McCartney, John, 41 Lucknow St.
	Prot.	McGrogan, Nellie, 30 Frome St.
26/7/20.	Prot.	Dunbar, Private David (20), 64 Sylvia St.
9/8/20.	Prot.	Parke, Private Matthew, 6 Lawther St

25/8/20.	Prot.	McCartney, James, Frome St. (Military fire, Newtownards Rd.)
	Prot.	Burrowes, Ethel Mary, 20 Bright St. (Military fire, Newtownards Rd.)
28/8/20.	Cath.	Burns, Terence (36), Massarene St.
29/8/20.	Cath.	Kinney, Henry, 120 Ardilea St.
	Cath.	Murray, John, 11 Glenview St.
	Cath.	Toner, Thomas (19), Ardilea St.
	Cath.	Moan, Owen, Glenview St.
	Cath	Cassidy, William J , Glenpark St.
	Cath.	Lynch, Robert (20), Massarene St.
	Cath.	Gilmore, Patrick, Campbell Row.
30/8/20.	Prot.	Hobson, Henry (19), 100 Cromwell Rd.
	Prot.	Thompson, John (18), Henry St.
	Prot.	M'Alpine, Robert (11), Lt. York St.
	Prot.	Coard, William (25), Lawther St.
	Prot.	M'Lean, Adam, 20 Southwell St.
	Prot.	Chapman, Paul, 16 Matilda St.
	Prot.	Orr, Grace, Edenderry St.
31/8/20.	Cath.	Burns, Edward, 65 Grove St.
	Prot.	Colville, Samuel, 16 Rowan St.
	Prot.	Jamison, Private, Scottish Rifles. (Shot in Orange quarter after curfew.)
	Prot.	Saye, Fred, 62 Donegall Pass. (Shot in Orange quarter after curfew.)
1/9/20.	Cath.	McCann, Henry, 34 Wall St.
	Cath.	Cromie, James, Trafalgar St.
	Prot.	Cawsard, James, 7 Benwell St.
	Prot.	Maxwell, Thomas, 61 N. Boundary St.
2/9/20.	Cath.	Hobbs, Fred, Boundary St.
	Prot.	Boyd, Thomas, Northland St.
3/9/20.	Prot.	McMurty, William (19), Derry St. R.V.H.
	Cath.	O'Brien, John (45), 9 Kildare St.
4/9/20.	Prot.	Harold, Charles, soldier, Military Hospital.
10/9/20.	Cath.	O'Neill, Charles (40), Glenpark St.
12/9/20.	Cath	Toner, John (58), 29 Cable St. (Shot during curfew)
	Prot.	Seymour, Robert, 186 Sandy Row.

20/9/20.   Prot.   Mathers, James D.. 18 Hartley St.
            Cath.   Leonard, Constable.

26/9/20.   Cath.   Trodden, Edward, 65 Falls Rd.
            Cath.   McFadden, John, 54 Springfield Rd.
            Cath.   Gaynor, James, 136 Springfield.

28/9/20.   Prot.   Blair, Fred, 69 Louisa St.

29/9/20.   Cath.   Gordon, Robert (18), 80 Falls Rd.
            Cath.   Barkley, Thomas (32), 38 Roumania St.
            Cath.   Shields, James (19), Milan St
            Cath.   Tier, William, 23 Mill St.
            Prot.   Lawther, John (19), 20 Everton St.

16/10/20.   Prot.   Gobson, John (55), Byron Pl.
            Prot.   Mitchell, William J. (25), 20 Downing St.

16/10/20.   Prot.   McMaster, Matthew (34), Conlig St. (Run
                    down by armoured car.)

25/10/20.   Prot.   McLeod, Joseph (25), 45 Church St., East.

4/11/20.   Prot.   McLean, John Cowan, Glenallen St.
            Prot.   Lucas, Sam. W., R.I.C.

21/11/20.   Prot.   Bundry, Arthur, soldier.

2/12/20.   Cath.   Bell, William (19), 100 Broom St.

3/12/20.   Cath.   Mullin, William, 99 Urney St.

27/12/20.   Prot.   Morrison, Joseph, 19 Boyne Sq.

1921

7/1/21.   Cath.   Horner, Daniel, 50 Kent St.

26/1/21.   Cath.   Heffron, Constable, Railway View Hotel.
            Cath.   Quinn, Constable, Railway View Hotel.
            Cath.   Garvey, Michael, Chemist, Crumlin Rd.

11/3/21.   Prot.   Crooks, R. E., Black-and-Tan.
            Prot.   McIntosh, John, Black-and-Tan.

25/2/21.	Prot.	Hepworth, Ambrose, Hill (Soldier from Oldergrove.)
	Prot.	Bray, E., Rosemount Gardens.
12/3/21.	Prot.	Alan, Alex. (50), Military Hospital. G.S.W.
13/3/21.	Prot.	Copper, Constable William (32), Black-and-Tan.
	Cath.	Graham, John, Emily Place.
22/3/21.	Cath.	Jamison, Annie, 10 Moffat St.
	Prot.	Boyd, Head Constable.
23/4/21.	Prot.	Bolan, Ernest, Auxiliary Police.
	Prot.	Bales, John B., Auxiliary Police.
	Cath.	Duffin, Patrick, 64 Clonard Gardens.
	Cath.	Duffin, Daniel, 64 Clonard Gardens.
17/5/21.	Cath.	Burns, Philomena (15), 24 Upton St.
22/5/21.	Cath.	Carroll, Mary Ann, Carntual St.
18/5/21.	Cath.	Smyth, John (29), Seaforde St.
19/5/21.	Cath.	Kelly, Eleanor Lena (13), Kilmood St.
11/5/21.	Prot.	Craig, Alfred (28), Ship St.
10/6/21.	Prot.	Glover, Constable James.
11/6/21.	Cath.	McGinley, Terence N., Thomas St.
13/6/21.	Cath.	Collins, Kathleen (18), Cupar St.
	Prot.	Frazer, James (12), Mayo St.
	Cath.	Mallon, Thomas N., Thomas St.
11/6/21.	Cath.	McBride, Alexander, Cliftonville Road.
	Cath.	Kerr, William, 47 Old Lodge Rd.
	Cath.	Halfpenny, Malachy, Hervert St., Ardoyne
	Prot.	Sturdy, Thomas (Sp. C.), Castlederg.
	Cath.	Milligan, Patrick (24), 2 Dock Lane.
	Cath.	Millar, Joseph (24), 2 New Dock St.
	Prot.	Jenkins, Edward (19), Emerson St.
14/6/21.	Cath.	McAree, Hugh (28), 12 Sackville St.
23/6/21.	Prot.	Blackburn, Joseph, 52 Hillman St.
6/7/21.	Cath.	Galvin, Jim, R.I.C.

10/7/21.	Cath.	Mulholland, Henry, 5 Bonbay St.
	Cath.	Lenaghan, James, 42 Lucan St.
	Cath.	Hughes, Daniel (50), Durham St.
	Cath.	Hickland, Patrick (38), Hamilton St.
	Cath.	Conlon, Constable Thomas (28), Springfield Rd. Barracks.
	Cath.	Hamilton, Ales. (21), 50 Plevna St.
	Prot.	Mullan, W. J., 51 James St.
	Prot.	McMullan, David (26), 58 Lawnbrook Avenue.
	Cath.	Robinson, Francis, 6 Brown St.
	Cath.	Monaghan, Bernard (about 90), 68 Abyssinia St.
	Cath.	Tierney, William (56), 16 Osman St.
	Cath.	McGuinness, James (36), 27 McMillan's Place.
		An Unknown Boy, aged 13 years.
	Prot.	Baxter, William John (12), 126 Argyle St.
	Prot.	Park, Ernest (16), 92 Moyola St.
10/7/21.	Cath.	Daniel Hughes (28), McCleery St.
11/7/21.	Cath.	Craig, James, 22 Turin St.
	Cath.	Ledlie, James (19), Plevna St.
14/7/21.	Cath.	McKenney, Maggie (26), 71 Bulkan St.
	Prot.	Welch, Maggie Ann (14), 2 Ellens Court.
	Cath.	McKenna, Patrick, Royal Victoria Hospital.
15/7/21.	Cath.	Mooney, Bernard (22), 104 Spamount St.
19/7/21.	Prot.	Brown, William (45), R. V., 30 March St.
21/7/21.	Prot.	Walker, George (19), 29 Eight St.
23/7/21.	Cath.	Magowan, Mary (13), Derby St.
15/8/21.	Cath.	Fox, Fred (19), Durham St.
25/8/21.	Prot.	Green, Charles S. (39), 23 Lincolin Avenue, R.V.
29/8/21.	Prot.	Rafter, Thomas (29), Lepper St.
	Prot.	Fogg, Colin, 35 Lowther St.

30/8/21.	Prot.	Barnes, Robert (22), 9 Cambridge St.
	Prot.	Kennedy, William (26), 8 Grove St.
	Prot.	Cash, Stephen, 77 Sussex St.
	Prot.	Watson, Annie (5), 177 North Queen St.
	Cath.	Harvey, Charles (39), Columbia St.
	Cath.	Coogan, John, 40 Valentia St.
	Prot.	Smith, William (28), Earl St.
	Prot.	Bowers, Henry, Cambridge St.
	Cath.	Mullan, Thomas, 84 North Queen St.
31/8/21.	Cath.	Bradley, James (24), 74 McCleery St.
	Cath.	Cuff, Alice (54), 67 Academy St.
	Cath.	Finnegan, Thomas, 5 Keystand Place.
	Cath.	McKeown, Wm. (18), 25 Thomas St.
	Prot.	Lee, John, Manor St.
	Prot.	Ferguson, Samuel (43), Donegall St.
	Cath.	Bradley, Frank, Boyd St.
	Prot.	Campbell, Walter (15), Silvio St.
	Cath.	Duffin, Richard, New Lodge Rd.
	Cath.	McFadden, James, 107 Malvern St.
6/9 21.	Cath.	Harvey, Charles (33), 31 Columbia St.
	Prot.	Leopold, Burgess Leonard (55), 5 Dover St.
18/9/21.	Prot.	Johnston, James (13), 19 Louisa St.
	Prot.	Ardis, Maggie (22), 7 Bute St.
	Prot.	Blair, Eva (23), 6 Vere St.
25 9/21.	Prot.	McMinn, F. S., Reids Place, Newtownards Rd.
	Prot.	Harrison, Alex., 20 Frazer St. (? Hamilton)
	Cath.	McAstocker, Murty (25), 5 Moira St.
	Cath.	Kelly, Eliza J., Mrs. (34), 67 Seaforde St.
	Cath.	Barry, George, 5 Shore St.
29/9/21.	Prot.	Orr, John (32), 84 Derwent St.
9/11/21.	Prot.	Blakely, Joseph (23), 32 Campbell St.
21/11/21.	Cath.	O'Hagan, James (22), Station St.
	Prot.	Hanna, William, Montrose St.
	Prot.	Stuart, Andrew J. (24), 126 Nelson St.
23/11/21.	Prot.	McPhillips, Bertie (25), Michael St.
	Prot.	Cunningham, David (19), 32 Lendrick St.
	Cath.	McConvey, Neil (55), Thompson St.
	Cath.	McConvey, Mrs. (56), Thompson St.
	Cath.	Kelly, Miss (20), Thompson St.

Cath,   Keating, J. P. (Clerk), Jocelyn Ave.
Prot.   McMordie, Wm. (Porter), 3 Sandhurst St.
Cath.   Malone, Patrick, Beersbridge Rd.
Cath.   Connolly, Patrick, 208 Duncairn Gardens.
Cath.   Brunton, Patrick (38), Vere St.
Cath.   Bell, Ellen (75), Lepper St.
Cath.   Spallen, Michael, 32 Moffett St.
Prot.   Patton, Andrew.
Cath,   McNally, John, 7 Park St.

24/11/21.   Prot.   Graham, Richard (45), Beverley St.
Cath.   Fleming, Jerh., Glenvale.
Cath.   Kelly, John, Crumlin Rd.
Prot.   Thompson, Thomas, Ohio St.
Cath.   Millar, Mrs., Dock L.

25/11/21.   Cath.   McIver, James, 54 Little Park St.
Prot.   Graham, Robert (48), 10 Beersbridge Rd.
Cath.   McHenry, John, Harbour Const.
Cath.   Kelly, Eugene, Crumlin Rd.

29/11/21.   Cath.   McNamara, Mrs., 56 Keegan St.

14/12/21.   Cath.   Crudden, Michael, Old Park Rd.

17/12/21.   Prot.   Pritchard, Walter, 9 Malcolm St.
Prot.   McMeigan, J., 35 Lower Mount St.
Cath.   Brennan, Edward (21), 44 Short Strand.

19/12/21.   Cath.   McCallion, Charles.
Cath,   Donnelly, Mrs., Ravenhill Rd.

27/12/21.   Cath.   Morrison, David, Ardoyne.

1922

1/1/22.   Wilson, John.

2/1/22.   Cath.   Corr, Hugh (14), Little Patrick St.
Prot.   Turtle, Alexander (22), Mountcollyer Rd.
Prot.   Barnes, Private, C. Coy., Norfolk Regt.
Prot.   Twittle, Alexander.
Cath.   Murphy, John, York St. (Shot in his own shop.)

3/1/22.   Cath.   Campbell, Saml. (1½).
Cath.   Gibbon, John, Arnon St.

4/1/22.	Prot.	McCrea, Albert, Roundhill St.
7/1/22.	Cath.	McDonagh, John (26), 24 Dock St.
8/1/22.	Cath.	Allwell, Wm. (19), Coates St.
11/1/22.	Prot.	Anderson, Andrew, Hooker St.
	Prot.	Anderson, Mrs., Hooker St.
	Cath.	Hogg, Mary (40), Fifth St.
	Cath.	Devlin, Mrs. Bridget, Coates St.
12/1/22.	Cath.	Kelly, Hugh (28), Barman Clarke, of Benterick St.
6/2/22.	Cath.	Gray, Thomas (19), Barman, Earl St.
11/2/22.	Cath.	Page, Mrs., 219 North Queen St.
	Prot.	Boyd, David (18), Stanhope St. area.
13/2/22.	Cath.	Neary, Francis, Peters St.
	Cath.	Gregg, James, Kildare St.
	Cath.	Mathers, James, Jude St.
	Prot.	Brown, James, Eighth St.
	Cath.	Lamb, Patrick, York St.
	Cath.	McNellis, Peter, Joy St.
		Brown, Joseph, Regent St.
	Cath.	Sadleir, Anthony, Tyrone St.
	Cath.	McNeill, Rose A., Mary St.
	Prot.	Lundy, Ben, Upper Meadow St.
	Cath.	Kennedy, Catherine, Weaver St.
	Cath.	Johnston, Mary (13), Weaver St.
	Cath.	Tennyson, W. (23), Cavendish St.
14/2/22.	Cath.	McCoy, Frank, 33 Forfar St.
	Prot.	Harper, George (16), Earl St.
	Prot.	Waring, William, Clifton St., Orange Hall.
	Cath.	Gallagher, Henry (40), Little Patrick St.
	Cath.	O'Hanlon, Eliza (11½), Weaver St.
	Prot.	Wallace, or Walls.
	Cath.	Rice, James (19), 20 Avondale St. (Hands tied, kicked, shot in ten places by twelve men.)
	Cath.	Robinson, Mary, Lancaster St.
	Prot.	Crothers, Joshua, 35 Ivan St.
	Prot.	McClelland, John, Christopher St. (carter).
	Prot.	Blair, Thomas (Saml.), (40), 63 Bainaby St.

15/2/22.   Prot.   Duffin, W. H., New North Spinning Co.
            Prot.   Law, James (Wm.), Hunter St.
            Cath.   Morrison, James (20), Sultan St.
            Cath.   McCall, Peter (22), 41 Tyrone St.
            Cath.   O'Brennan, Mrs., My Lady's Road.
            Prot.   Stewart, Hector, " B " Special, Ship St.
            Prot.   Ffrench, Hugh, Old Lodge Rd.
            Cath.   Bond, Owen, Stanfield St.
            Prot.   Neale, Thomas, Peveril St.

16/2/22.   Cath.   Devlin, John (5), Hiddleston Place.
            Prot.   McCormick, James.

24/2/22.   Cath.   Reilly, James (W.), Old Lodge Rd.
            Prot.   Hardy, Edward, Brookhill Avenue.
            Prot.   Hutton, James (45), 27 Central St.

26/2/22.   Prot.   MacMillan, Isaac.
            Cath.   Hughes, James (23), 315 Crumlin Rd.
            Cath.   McMullan, Charles (49), Sherwood St.

27/2/22.   Prot.   Fry, David, or Fryer, McClure St.

4/3/22.   Cath.   Hughes, Owen (20), Skegoniel St.
            Prot.   Martin, James R., Clerk, Midland Railway.
6/3/22.   Cath.   Eastwood, Thomas, Upton St.
            Cath.   Lynch, Catherine (51), Letitia St.

7/3/22.   Cath.   Thompson, James, 31 Kane St.
            Cath.   Mullan, John, Wall St.
            Prot.   Waider, Wm. (16), 19 Lower Urney St.
            Prot.   Morrison, John, 34 Gardiner St.

8/3/22.   Prot.   Johnson, W., Cavour St.
            Cath.   Duffy, Stewart, Garmoyle St.
            Prot.   Hazard, R. (24).

9/3/22.   Prot.   Roddy, John, Broadbent St.
            Cath.   Morgan, Patrick (58), Upton St.

10/3/22.   Cath.   Kerr, Wm. J., Mountpleasant, Whitehouse.
            Cath.   Connor, Patrick, Constable, R.I.C., Spring-
                         field Rd.
            Cath.   Cullen, John, Constable, R.I.C., Spring-
                         field Rd.
            Prot.   Bruce, Lieut., Seaforth Highlanders.

11-12/3/22. Cath.   Neeson, or Eason, Catherine (27), Little
                     George St. Baby of 7 months delivered
                     dead.
            Cath.   Leith, Benedict (23), Regent St.
            Prot.   Woods, Herbert (26), California St.
            Cath.   McNally, Hugh (34), 8 Maple Terrace.
            Cath.   Murphy, Terence (2½), Harthley St.
            Prot.   Vokes, Charles (38), Upper Meadow St.,
                     " A " Special.
                     Keyes, Sarah (35), 117 Hillman St.

13/3/22.   Cath.   Clarke, Sergt., R.I.C.
            Cath.   Leonard, Andrew (21), Duffy St.

15/3/22.   Cath.   Wilson, Mary (4), 57 Norfolk St.
            Cath.   Rooney, Patrick (24), Corporation St.

16/3/22.   Cath.   Kane, Wm. (50), Dunmurry (Van Driver).
            Prot.   Taylor, John (64), Duncairn Gardens.

18-19/3/22. Cath.   Orange, Agustus (24), Ravenhill Rd.
            Cath.   Mullen, Mary (40), Thompson St.
            Prot.   Murphy, Margaret, Campbell St.
                     (Husband Catholic).
            Prot.   Garvey, Henry Martin.
            Prot.   Devaney, Alex., Church St., E.
            Cath.   Rogan, Daniel, Lincoln St.

20/3/22.   Cath.   Magee, James, 11 Harding St.
            Cath.   Hillis, James (23), 8 Nail St., Falls Rd.
            Prot.   Harkness, John (24), 14 Lackagh St.

22/3/22.   Cath.   Mullen, Thomas, 67 Short Strand.
            Cath.   Kerney, John, Young's Row.

23/3/22.   Prot.   Cunningham, Thomas, Josford St., Ormeau
                     Road, Special.
            Prot.   Chermside, William (31), Josford St.,
                     Ormeau Rd., Special.

24/3/22.   Cath.   McMahon, Owen (57), Father.
            Cath.   McMahon, Jerh. (15½), Son.
            Cath.   McMahon, Patrick (22), Son.
            Cath.   McMahon, Francis (23), Son.
            Cath.   McKinney, Edward.
            Prot.   Campbell, William, 33 Old Park Rd.
            Cath.   Fitzsimons, Patrick (20), 5 Frederick St.

26/3/22.	Cath.	McGreevy, Mrs. Rose (80).
	Prot.	Allen, William J., 4 Sackville Place.
	Prot.	Bell, John, My Lady's Road.
	Prot.	McGarry, John, Glenwherry St.
	Cath.	Savage, Maggie (21), Barker St.
	Cath.	Magee, Jas., MacDonnell St.
	Prot.	Brennan, H., Donegall Road.
		Nesson, I., Roumania St.
30/3/22.	Cath.	Dempsey, Jack, Mountcollyer Avenue.
31/3/22.	Prot.	Hale, Thomas (Special Constable).
	Cath.	Sweeney, John, Stanhope St.
1-2/4/22.	Prot.	Turner, J., Constable, R.I.C., Brown Sq. Barracks.
	Cath.	McKenna, Bernard (36), Park St.
	Cath.	McRory, John (40), Stanhope St.
	Cath.	Spallen, William (63), 16 Arnon St.
	Cath.	Walsh, Joseph (39), 18 Arnon St.
	Cath.	Walsh, Robert, 3 Alton St.
	Cath.	Mallon, John, Grove Back Lodge, Skegoniel Avenue.
4/4/22.	Cath.	McMahon, Joseph (26) (of the McMahon Family).
	Prot.	Donnelly, Joseph (12), 29 Brown St.
	Prot.	Donnelly, Francis (2½), 29 Brown St.
6/4/22	Cath.	Hannigan, Joseph (9), 27 Maralin St.
	Cath.	Owens, Mary, Shore St. (Victim of Weaver St. bomb.)
14/4/22.	Prot.	Carmichael, Matthew, 20 Moyola St.
	Cath.	Beattie, Danl., 65 Herbert St.
	Prot.	Sloan, John, 20 Harrison St.
	Cath.	Gillan, Thomas, Engine Driver, Midland Railway.
	Prot.	Cowan, William (5), 131 Templemore St.
18/4/22.	Prot.	Johnston, William (27), 100 Louisa St.
	Cath.	Fearson, James (56), 22 Glenpark St.
	Cath.	McGoldrick, Patrick, 27 Madrid St.
19/4/22.	Cath.	Hobbs, Francis, 26 Kilmood St.
	Cath.	Berry, Mary A., 17 Arran St.
	Cath.	Dougan, Rose, 15 Arran St.
	Prot.	Scott, John (16), 15 Well St.

20/4/22.	Prot.	Johnston, James (50), My Lady's Road.
	Cath.	Bruen, Sergeant, Henry St. Barracks.
	Cath.	Keenan, Mary (13), Marine St.
	Cath.	Walker, John (16), 97 Short Strand.
	Cath.	Diamond, Danl. (25), 50 Vulcan St.
	Cath.	McCartney, Andrew, 22 Dagmar St.
21/4/22.	Prot.	Best, Thomas (18), Louisa St.
	Prot.	Greer, James, Lower Frank St.
24/4/22.	Cath.	Corr, James, 33 Lowry St.
	Port.	Sibbison, William, 1 Havelock Place, Ormeau Rd.
23/4/22.	Cath.	McCabe, Mrs., 45 Seaforde St.
	Prot.	Millar, R., Beechfield St.
24/4/22.	Prot.	Steele, W., Disraeli St.
	Prot.	Greer, Ellen, Enniskillen St.
12/5/22.	Cath.	Cullen, Michael (44), 27 Havanna St.
	Prot.	Mansfield, John, Tram Conductor.
13-14/5/22.	Cath.	Douglas, Kathleen (13), 38 Marine St.
	Prot.	Beattie, Robert, 8 Palmer St.
	Prot.	McAlorey, Lizzie, 3 Melbourne Court.
	Cath.	Dargan, Ellen, 10 Emily Place.
16/5/22.	Cath.	Madden, Wm. Owen (22), Sackville St.
17/5/22.	Cath.	Gribben, John (21), Gordon St.
18/5/22.	Cath.	McPeake, Sam., Ligoniel Rd.
	Cath.	Donaghy, James, Ligoniel Place.
	Cath.	McCaffrey, Thomas, 43 Shore St.
	Cath.	Collins, Constable.
	Prot.	McKnight, Wm. G., McTier St.
19/5/22.	Prot.	Paterson, Wm., Frazer St.
	Prot.	Boyd, Thomas, 36 Louisa St.
	Prot.	Maxwell, Thomas, Durham St.
	Prot.	Heslip, Constable.
	Prot.	Donaldson, Mary, 220 Spamount St.

20/5/22.	Cath.	Connolly, John, 7 New Lodge Place.
	Cath.	McAuley, Patrick (18), 4 Ton St.
	Cath.	McGuigan, Thomas (18), 95 Stanfield St.
	Cath.	McMorrogh, Arthur, Grosvenor Place.
	Cath.	McDermott, Francis, 28 Lady St.
	Cath.	Skillen, Brigid (3), 26 Herbert St.
	Cath.	Condit, Agnes (22), 58 Fleet St.
	Cath.	Kearns, Cecilia, 171 York St.
	Cath.	McShane, Thomas, 5 Jennymount St.
	Cath.	Hickey, John, 17 Nelson St.
	Cath.	Murtagh, Joseph, Palmer St.
	Prot.	Newell, Robert, 14 Clonallen St.
	Cath.	McDonald, Hugh, 5 Saul St.
22/5/22.	Cath.	McLarnon, 61 Moyola St.
	Cath.	McMurty, Charles, Trades Hotel.
	Cath.	Brady, James, 9 Kilmood St.
	Prot.	Twaddell, W. J., M.P., Malone Park.
	Prot.	Boyd, Thomas, 208 Donegall Rd.
	Prot.	Lawson, George, Maymount St.
23/5/22.	Cath.	Grant, Mary Ann, Fleet St.
	Prot.	Powell, Robert, Isabella St.
24/5/22.	Prot.	Telford, James, 21 Broadway.
	Prot.	Moore, John (17), 79 Hooker St.
	Cath.	O'Hare, Jack, Thompson St.
	Prot.	Kidd, Victor, 44 Brookvale Avenue.
25/5/22.	Cath.	McDougall, Esther, 11 Stanhope St.
	Cath.	Hughes, Patrick, Carntall St.
	Prot.	Murphy, Special Constable.
	Prot.	Shiels, William (19), 32 Delaware St.
	Prot.	Connor, George, Special Constable.
26/5/22.	Prot.	Morrison, Alexander, Ballyclare.
	Prot.	Campbell, Georgina (10), 5 Roxburgh St.
	Cath.	Toal, William (17), 42 Mayfair St.
27-28/5/22.	Cath.	Rainey, Robert, Cyprus St.
	Cath.	William, Smyth (21), Moira St.
	Prot.	Todd, Grace, 25 Bedeque St.
29/5/22.	Cath.	Drumgoale, Thomas, Seaforde St.
	Cath.	Hughes, Francis, Varna St.
	Prot.	McGarety, Special Constable.
	Prot.	Boyd, Minnie, Wilson St.
30/5/22.	Cath.	O'Brien, Henry, Constable.

31/5/22.	Cath.	Monaghan, Robert, Arizona St.
	Prot.	Collum, W. H., 13 Portallo St.
	Cath.	McIlroy, Maryann, Old Lodge Road.
	Cath.	McIlroy, Rose (Daughter), Old Lodge Road.
	Cath.	Kennedy, Hugh, 98 Servia St.
	Cath.	O'Hara, William, Montgomery St.
	Prot.	Rouleston, Special Constable.
	Cath.	Doran, Jane, Peter's Place.
	Prot.	Jennings, John, Peter's Place.
	Cath.	McGurk, Patrick, Ardmoulin Avenue.
	Cath.	McGahey, George (17), Irwin St.
1/6/22.	Cath.	McHugh, Michael, 137 New Lodge Rd.
	Prot.	Kane, James F., Limestone Rd.
	Prot.	McMordie, Albert (11), Lower Urney St.
2/6/22.	Cath.	Donnelly, Lizzie, West St.
	Prot.	Kane, John (16), D'Israeli St.
3/5/22.	Cath.	Black, John, New Dock St.
	Cath.	Hunt, Robert, 14 Milford St.
	Cath.	McCaffrey, Bernard (16), N. Lodge Rd.
		Rice, William (25), Fairview St.
5/5/22.	Cath.	Gough, Thomas, 17 Mineral St.
6/6/22.	Cath.	O'Malley, Patrick, Stratheden St.
7/6/22.	Cath.	McMenermy, John, 58 Conway St.
12/6/22.	Cath.	Devine, Edward D., Springfield Rd.
13/6/22.	Cath.	Smyth, William, Hardinge St.
16/6/22.	Cath.	Mullaney, Thomas, East St.
20/6/22.	Cath.	O'Neill, Charles, Plevna St.
	Cath.	Teuton, James, Brookfield St.
21/6/22.	Cath.	Ward, P. J.
	Cath.	Millar, William, Willowfield St.
	Cath.	Johnston, Thomas, 28 Frederick St.
23/6/22.	Cath.	Rea, Leo (16.)
	Prot.	Kirkwood, William, Lisburn Rd.
	Cath.	Joseph Hurson (15), 87 Unity St.
	Prot.	Semple, Mary (25), 61 Ardgowan St.
24/6/22.	Prot.	Young, Isabella (½), Ballyclare St.

It will be observed that the number of Catholics on the foregoing list is much larger than the number of Protestants. Of the latter, a big proportion were the victims of military fire. The Orange party, being nearly always the aggressors, were often made to pay the penalty of such aggression. No doubt, many of those who suffered were quite inoffensive people.; but in the chief areas of the disturbance the Protestants were mostly in a majority of at least six to one, and it is very remarkable that they did not suffer heavier losses, considering the vast amount of shooting rather wildly indulged in by the Crown Forces and their own party, not to mention anyone else. It would, of course, be ridiculous to deny that many of them were shot by Catholics in the various frays, but probably these did not amount to a half. The following well-informed extract from the *Weekly Irish Bulletin* of June 19, 1922, is worth quoting :

" Of the ninety-six Protestants killed since 1st January the first name on the list is Alex. Turtle of Mountcollyer Road. He was an Orange sniper killed by the military on the 2nd January. On the 8th March, Herbert Hazard, of 16, Earl Lane, was lying flat on the street sniping into a street where Catholic children were playing about. An eye-witness has made an affidavit that she saw a soldier come up behind him and, seeing what he was, fired a shot. Hazard thereupon rolled over stone dead. At his funeral the Orange gunmen shot up Greencastle and killed and wounded several people. He was represented by the Orange Press as another victim of Sinn Fein gunmen. On March 12th the military arrested a man in Royal Avenue. They deprived him of his revolver.   On the way to the barracks he tried to escape but was shot dead.   That man was Special Constable Vokes, a native of Ballymena.   Vokes was evidently out on a criminal business.   On the 14th April Mat. Carmichael and John Sloan were shot (according to the Belfast Press) ' under mysterious circumstances.'   In other words, they were shot in the worst Orange portion of Belfast in mistake for Catholics.   On the 18th April William Johnston, 100, Louisa Street, was shot by military; Thomas Best, Louisa Street, was shot accidentally by the military. On 24th April William Steele, Disraeli Street, was shot accidentally, as was Ellen Greer, of Enniskillen Street, who was killed by a revolver belonging to her brother-in-law, an ' A.' Special.   Mary Donaldson of Spamount Street was killed by military on the 19th May, as was Robert Dudgeon, of 74, Westland Street. On the 24th May John Moore, 79, Hooker Street, was shot by an Orange sniper and on the same day Victor Kidd, 44, Brookvale Avenue, was shot by military. On the 25th May William Shields, 32, Delaware Street, was shot by a Protestant sniper.   Alex. Morrison, Ballyclare, was shot in the Albert Bridge Road by an Orange murder gang.   (Fourteen Catholics have now been done to death at this spot by Orange murderers).   John Jennings, a blind and paralysed old man lodged with Jane Doran, a Catholic, at Peter's Place.   During the terror on the 31st May, an Orange mob of ' Specials ' and hooligans threw a bomb into this house.   This bomb killed the residents.   The remains of the blind Protestant and his Catholic landlady were subsequently found by the Fire Brigade.   The bulk of the remaining Protestants were shot by ' Specials ' in the course of indiscriminate firing.   A few undoubtedly have been shot by desperate avengers of Catholic victims.

" Of the 203 Protestants wounded the same may be said.   Five of them were ' Specials ' who were shot while attempting another massacre of Catholics."

APPENDICES

LETTERS FROM *Belfast News Letter* PROFESSING
TO SHOW THAT THE RAPID GROWTH OF
CATHOLICISM IN THE NORTH-EAST WAS A
MENACE TO PROTESTANTISM AND GIVING
STRAIGHT HINTS AS TO THE REMEDY.

News Letter, 15th July, 1920 (six days before
pogram) :

LETTER TO THE EDITOR.

" SIR,—I notice that in his great speech on the
Twelfth Sir Edward Carson made one statement
which, if I may be permitted to say so, is far from
accurate. He says that the Roman Catholics make
very little progress in Ulster. Now I certainly think
this is a serious error and the very worst false security
into which the Protestants could be lulled. In my
opinion, the progress made by the Roman Catholics
in Ulster is extraordinarily rapid and extensive. Take
the village where I live, for instance, which is one of
the most Protestant communities of Ulster. There
is a population of about 1000. Some thirty years
ago it was an entirely Protestant village without, I
believe, one single Roman Catholic inhabitant. Now
nearly one-half of the inhabitants are Catholics, and
they are increasing rapidly. This is only one instance
of many. And look at Londonderry city. The
increase of population there has been so considerable

as to give them the government of the ancient city and fortress of Protestantism. One should look facts in the face. The Roman Catholics are pouring into Ulster and increasing rapidly in this province where Protestants are emigrating and disappearing. It seems to me that in a comparatively short number of years the majority of Ulster's inhabitants will undoubtedly be Roman Catholics, if things go on as at present. After looking facts in the face, and not ignoring them because they may be unpleasant, the next thing to do is to counter them energetically in every possible way. I have several plans by which this could, and should, be done, but the question is whether Protestants can rouse themselves to do anything apart from processions, which I greatly doubt, as a post-war apathy or sleeping sickness seems to have spread over the whole of Ulster Unionism which it is highly necessary should be cured before it gets much worse. This is not only my opinion. Ulster Unionists in general are not what they were before the War. There is a lamentable change. Things go on in Ulster now which would never have been permitted, or been possible, in early 1914. Had the Sinn Feiners then attacked the Unionists in Londonderry, I believe that Unionists would have arisen from all parts of Ulster in their thousands and gone to the rescue and assistance of their own people there. I think it is disgraceful this was not done, and that the brave Londonderry Protestants had to defend themselves alone as best they could. They have my admiration and my sympathy. The old 1914 fighting spirit is still alive in them. But the apathy and stagnation—to use no worse adjective—amongst the rest of the Unionists in Ulster is deplorable. Some time ago Sir Edward Carson gave out a call to revive the Unionists' Clubs. After a very brief and feeble existence they are now evidently dead and buried. In a recent speech Sir Edward Carson said that Ulster Unionists would not permit disorder or lawlessness, etc., in their province. Since then plenty of outrages, etc., and flagrant lawlessness have taken place in Ulster, and no Unionists had either organised or attempted to do anything in the matter. It is time that Unionists roused themselves to act, because before very long it will not be possible to do anything. With your permission I could suggest much that should be done.—Yours,

" OBSERVER.

" 14th July, 1920."

Belfast News Letter, 16th July, 1920 :

LETTERS TO EDITOR.

ROMAN CATHOLICS IN ULSTER.

" SIR,—It was with much interest I read ' Observer's ' letter which appeared in your columns of the 15th inst. I can heartily endorse everything that your correspondent says in his letter, and I am afraid it is only too true that our Ulster Unionism is at present suffering from ' sleeping sickness.' ' Observer's ' statement that ' the progress made by Roman Catholics in Ulster is extraordinarily rapid and extensive ' is absolutely accurate, as everyone who will take the trouble to ascertain the facts must know. We Protestants should ask ourselves how is it that Roman Catholics have made such headway in our midst? I think if we did we should not have any difficulty in finding the answer. We are up against an insidious system of ' peaceful penetration' which has, to my mind, too long taken advantage of our fear of being called ' bigoted.' Londonderry city is a standing example of what our toleration has led to. Loyalists employ over 80 per cent. of the labour of that city, the bulk of this being composed of Roman Catholics, be they Nationalists or Sinn Feiners. The result of this well-intentioned but foolish policy on the part of Unionists there has, unfortunately, been very forcibly and ruthlessly brought home to them for a few weeks past.

' Observer ' rightly states that it is time Unionists roused themselves to action, and I quite agree with him that unless we do so without delay we shall be left homeless and helpless very shortly. What, I would ask, are our Ulster organisations doing to combat this menace of ' peaceful penetration '? Processions and demonstrations are all very good in their own way, but we want something deeper than these. We know the powerful organisation behind this ' New Plantation,' as I have heard it called; and I feel confident that if Ulster Protestants but rouse themselves from their lethargy we will have little difficulty in dealing with this latest device to drive out the British garrison. I, like ' Observer,' might suggest much that could be done. In the meantime I have no doubt that our leaders have this question before them. Let them not hesitate to ask us to take whatever steps they consider necessary to counter this present movement. The old spirit which existed in 1914 is still alive in Ulster—it only needs wakening.—Yours truly,

" THOR.

" Belfast, 15th July, 1920."

" SIR,—Having read ' Observer's ' letter in to-day's issue, I quite agree with him that, if work (not talk) is not begun at once, it is only a matter of a very short time and Protestantism will be wiped out of this country altogether. Take the church reports, and what do you find? Amalgamations taking place not only in the South and West, but in Ulster counties. I know where recently a minister has been appointed where formerly three were required to do the work of the three parishes. I know where schools have even closed for want of children to keep the average up. I know districts where some years ago three or four strong Orange Lodges worked now hardly able to keep one, or at most two, in working order, while in these districts new and larger Roman Catholic churches and schools are being erected, or extensions to the existing ones. Hibernian and Sinn Fein halls are being built to accommodate their ever-increasing numbers, and, having captured County, District and Urban Councils in the late contests, all appointments under their control will in future go to Roman Catholics. I believe that those who say Protestantism is prosperous—even in this province—are wilfully closing their eyes to realities. What an eye-opener the next Census returns will produce! Canon Austin, in the cathedral on Sunday evening, saw clearly where events were leading, and his text (Rev. iii. 2) to my mind was most applicable to the situation that exists regarding Protestantism in this province at the present time. Like 'Observer,' I, too, could suggest much that should be done, but I go further and say that we have done things we should not have done, and, unless our leaders apply themselves to the problem that faces them, we can only expect defeat.—Yours,

'' PROTESTANT.''

FURTHER LETTER TO EDITOR.

'' SIR,—' Observer,' in his very able letter, has struck the right note. The Protestants of Ulster are asleep while the Sinn Feiners, who are pouring into our province, are wide awake; they are busy organising, while we prate of the deeds of our forefathers and do nothing ourselves. To the shame of the Ulster Unionists be it said that Sinn Feiners can obtain situations in both offices and shipyards, in so-called loyal Belfast, while our Protestant men walk about idle. They can get houses while Protestants are herded two or three families in one small house. They are allowed to buy up property in town and country. Ulster is well planted by rebels from the South and West.—Yours,

'' H. S.

'' 15th July, 1920.''

II.

STATISTICS SHOWING THE ABSOLUTE AND RELATIVE DECLINE OF CATHOLICITY IN ULSTER GOING ON STEADILY FOR OVER SIXTY YEARS

ULSTER.

Year	Catholics	Per cent.	Episc. Protestants	Per cent.	Presbyterians	Per cent.	Methodists	Per cent.	Others	Per cent.	TOTAL
1861 ...	966,613	50.5	391,315	20.4	503,835	26.3	32,030	1.7	20,443	1.1	1,914,236
1871 ...	897,230	48.9	393,268	21.5	477,729	26.1	29,903	1.6	35,098	1.9	1,833,228
1881 ...	833,566	47.8	379,402	21.8	451,629	25.9	34,825	2.0	43,653	2.5	1,743,075
1891 ...	744,859	46.0	362,791	22.4	426,245	26.3	40,526	2.5	45,391	2.8	1,619,814
1901 ...	699,202	44.18	360,373	22.77	425,526	26.88	47,372	2.99	50,353	3.18	1,582,826
1911 ...	690,816	43.67	366,773	23.19	421,410	26.64	48,816	3.09	53,881	3.41	1,581,696

CITY OF BELFAST.

Year	Catholics	Per cent.	Episc. Protestants	Per cent.	Presbyterians	Per cent.	Methodists	Per cent.	Others	Per cent.	TOTAL
1861 ...	41,406	33.9	30,080	24.6	42,604	35.2	4,946	4.1	2,566	2.2	121,602
1871 ...	55,575	31.9	46,423	26.6	60,249	34.5	6,775	3.9	5,390	3.1	174,412
1881 ...	59,957	28.8	58,410	28.1	71,521	34.4	9,141	4.4	9,075	4.3	208,122
1891 ...	67,378	26.3	75,522	29.5	87,234	34.1	13,747	5.4	12,069	4.7	255,950
1901 ...	85,992	24.34	102,991	29.5	120,269	34.44	21,506	6.16	19,422	5.56	349,180
191I ...	93,243	24.10	118,173	30.54	130,575	33.74	23,782	6.15	21,174	5.47	386,947

III.

CATHOLICS IN THE PUBLIC SERVICES OF BELFAST.

ACCORDING to the Census of 1891 Catholics numbered 26·3 per cent. of the population of Belfast. In 1892 a Select Committee was appointed to collect evidence in connection with the Belfast Corporation, Lunatic Asylums, etc. Bill then before the British House of Commons. In the Minutes of Evidence we find the following figures :

(1892).

	CORPORATION	
	Protestants	*Catholics*
Members	40	0
Paid Officials	89	2
	HARBOUR BOARD	
Members	22	0
Paid Officials	37	0
	WATER COMMISSION	
Members	15	1
Paid Officials	7	0
	POOR LAW BOARD	
Members	43	1
Paid Officials	91	3
	ASYLUM BOARD	
Members	19	3
Paid Officials	65	8
	PETTY SESSIONS CLERKS	
Members	—	—
Paid Officials	6	0
Protestant total	434	
Catholic total		18

181

These figures need no commentary except, perhaps, this—that the eight Catholic officials in the asylum were mere attendants, and that the two in the pay of the Corporation drew between them £265 a year.

(1896).

The figures for 1896 were :

	CORPORATION	
	Protestants	*Catholics*
Members	40	0
Paid Officials	95	2
Salaries	£18,467	£294
	POOR LAW BOARD	
Members	38	3
Paid Officials	164	6
Salaries	£10,223	£170
	WATER COMMISSION	
Members	17	0
Salaries	£3,524	0
	HARBOUR BOARD	
Members	22	0
Salaries	£7,648	£130

Before the Select Committee on the Belfast Corporation Bill, 1896, Mr. W. J. Pirrie, the Lord Mayor, admitted that there was an annual expenditure of about £144,000 for contractors, and that not one of these was a Catholic, though the Catholics contributed about £30,000 a year in rates. It was also admitted before the same Committee that in the course of fifty years only three Catholics had been elected to the Corporation.

(1922).

From the Minutes of the Belfast Corporation for March 1, 1922, the following figures have been extracted and certified for us :

Total of paid officials, 681.
Number of Catholics, 33.
Total of salaries, £17,223 3s. od.
Salaries to Catholics, £637 12s. od.

That means that only 4·85 per cent. of the paid officials are Catholics and that these receive only 3·7 per cent. of the money expended. Now, at the last Census (1911), the Catholics numbered 24·10 of the population of Belfast.

In this connection an interesting case occurred last February. The Belfast Public Libraries advertised three vacancies for Junior Assistants. Over 100 presented themselves and were examined by the Technical Institute. The results forwarded to the Library and Technical Committee of the Corporation were these : First place, a Catholic ; second place, a Protestant ; third and fourth places, Catholics. The Committee, however, ruled out the first on the list, a Catholic, and took the second on the list, a Protestant ; ruled out the third and fourth, who were Catholics, and selected the fifth and ninth, who were Protestants. It may be added that the three Catholic boys brushed aside, although they secured first, third and fourth places, were of distinctly good manner, personal appearance and character. " I would as soon trust a number of lambs before a jury of butchers, as trust Catholic interests to the Belfast Corporation,'' remarked Mr. Devlin in the British House of Commons, May 9, 1919.

From the Financial Statement of the Belfast Union for half-year ended March 31, 1920, we take the following figures :

PERMANENT OFFICIALS

Protestants	Catholics
170	19

SALARIES

£20,704	£1,102

Catholics, therefore, receive 10 per cent. of the salaried positions, but only 5 per cent. of the monies.

We have not been able to secure the Minutes of the other Public Bodies of Belfast ; but the attitude of its one-year-old Parliament towards the Catholics is revealed in the following extract from the *Freeman* of September 5, 1921 :

"The policy of the North-Eastern Parliament in regard to the religious complexion of the appointments to be made in the various departments under its jurisdiction is now unmistakably manifest. Many incidents have arisen during the negotiations for the transfer of Dublin Civil Servants to Belfast which make it clear that it is a case of 'No Catholic need apply.'

"The public is already well aware of the criticisms that have been passed on Mr. Archdale, Minister of Agriculture, for having arranged to appoint as his chief officer a Catholic. Only last week we published particulars of another case in which all the Irish applicants for a particular position were Catholics. In order to avoid the necessity of appointing one of them, the Minister concerned brought a man over specially from England to fill the post, in the belief, of course, that this man was a Protestant. To his dismay he has now discovered that the official is a Catholic, with the result that the Minister is in a sea of trouble with the McGuffins, Cootes and others of their class.

" Some further incidents of the same kind have also come to our notice. One is that of a prominent official of a Dublin department who went to Belfast recently on the instructions of his chief to discuss the question of transfers from his department. He brought with him a list of officers proposed to be transferred and submitted it to ————. The latter said he was sorry to have to ask him one question, namely, the respective religions of the officials on the list. The Dublin official gave the information required, and immediately the names of the Catholic Civil Servants were struck out.

" It is further stated that the head of another department in Dublin was bluntly informed that he would be only wasting his time in including Catholics in any list of officials he submitted for transfer to Belfast.

" The conclusion is inevitable that this wholesale exclusion of Catholics is not merely the policy of the Orange groundlings, but is the adopted policy of Sir James Craig and his Cabinet."

IV.

A CONTRAST.

PROTESTANT TESTIMONY TO THE TOLERANCE AND KINDNESS OF THE CATHOLIC MAJORITY IN THE SOUTH AND WEST OF IRELAND.

From countless similar declarations, coming from every corner of Catholic Ireland and beyond, we take the following :

"Amidst all the fearful scenes that have lately been perpetrated in our land by armed gangs of men, it is a notable fact that nowhere has a hand been raised against one of our isolated church buildings nor against a single individual Presbyterian as such in the South and West."—Right Rev. Dr. Glenn, outgoing Moderator of the Presbyterian Church in Ireland, at Belfast, June 8th, 1921.

"As far as I know, in a country place in Ireland there has never been any interference, good or bad or indifferent, with the worship of Methodists. The courtesy and kindness shown to your representatives in Ireland are more than tongue can tell. I am as hopeful of Ireland as ever man could be."—Mr. Ernest Mercier, Lay Representative of the Irish Methodist Conference at Hull, July 16, 1920.

"During my experience of over thirty years in the County Galway, I have not only never had the slightest disrespect shown to me or to those belonging to me as Protestants, but from the priests and people, gentle and simple, have received the utmost consideration and friendship."—Rev. I. C. Trotter, Protestant Rector, Ardrahan, County Galway.— *Irish Times,* 23rd July, 1920.

The long series of atrocities very briefly touched upon in the preceding pages, and culminating after nearly two years in the butchery of whole Catholic families, brought forth a vigorous, if tardy, outcry from many quarters.

From numberless places in the South and West, the Protestants, grateful for the kindness they had always received from their Catholic neighbours, raised a chorus of condemnation, in the Press and by public meeting, against the Belfast atrocities. We append a few of those outspoken declarations, taken chiefly from the Unionist Press :

"At a meeting of the Protestants of Limerick County and City yesterday, at which Sir Charles Barrington, Vice-Lieutenant of the County, presided,

" The Chairman, who announced that he had called the meeting on behalf of Lord Dunraven, said that the question of religion never arose in Limerick or the South, where they all, Catholic and Protestant, lived in the best of harmony and good-fellowship. They all appreciated toleration, and reciprocated the kindly feelings shown them by their Catholic fellow-countrymen. (Applause).

" Mr. W. Waller, D.L., said that any sort of religious tyranny was abhorrent. Murder and cruelty were hateful, and, when committed in the guise of religion, were the worst form of tyranny. Political passion in Belfast had been very much in evidence for many years past, but the present horrors in that city were of a character that were not known before. They were of a character that had shocked the whole community, the attack on, and the murder of, the McMahon family being the worst ever heard of. They had seen the letter of Sir Henry Wilson on the situation in the North. That letter, he had no hesitation in saying, was written for a political purpose—(applause)—because it asserted that the

Protestants of the South were not allowed to conduct their business in an ordinary manner. The Protestants were a small, a very small, minority of the population of Southern Ireland, and had always been treated with the utmost toleration and respect in the twenty-six counties, where they carried on their business without interference in any way, and lived in the best and most friendly relations with their Catholic fellow-countrymen.

" Mr. A. Murray, in seconding the resolution, said that he had lived all his lifes amongst his Roman Catholic fellow-countrymen in Limerick and elsewhere, and had never received anything but the utmost kindness and consideration at their hands.

" Captain Delmege said that it was a gross outrage to have it circulated that the Protestant minority were ill-treated, when the fact was that they received nothing but kindness, courtesy and goodwill at the hands of their Catholic fellow-countrymen. (Applause)."—From *Irish Times*, 5th April, 1922.

" At a meeting of Protestants held in the Constitutional Club, Sligo, yesterday, a resolution, which expressed abhorrence at the murders committed in Belfast, and particularly the murder of the McMahon family, was adopted.

" Mr. Arthur Jackson, D.L., who presided, said that he was sure that many of their co-religionists in Belfast abhorred murders as much as they did. Those present at that meeting lived in a community where the majority differed from them in religion and politics, and, although Ireland was passing through the greatest political upheaval in its history, not one Protestant had been injured in Sligo."—*Irish Times*, 30th March, 1922.

" We have received a statement signed by forty-eight Protestants living in Killarney and district, which says:

"We desire to join with our fellow-Protestants in condemning the cruel murders perpetrated on the McMahons and other families in the North, which have filled us with deep grief and horror, remembering the harmony and good feeling which have always existed between ourselves and our Roman Catholic fellow-countrymen; and we hereby denounce sectarian strife of all kinds and long to see complete unity."—*Irish Times* (Protestant), 1st April, 1922.

"At a large and representative meeting of Athlone Protestants, the Rev. J. H. Rice, B.D., the Rector of St. Mary's, presiding, the following resolution was unanimously passed:

"That we, the Protestants of Athlone, in meeting assembled, desire to put on record our abhorrence of the murders and atrocities committed in Belfast. We have always lived on the friendliest terms with our Catholic neighbours in Athlone, and we feel that, if we are to have a happy and prosperous country, all Irishmen must co-operate to drive bigotry and intolerance from our midst."—*Evening Mail,* 1st April, 1922.

"At a meeting of Protestants of the town of Portarlington, held on April 5, it was unanimously decided to join in condemning, in the strongest terms, the cruel murders perpetrated throughout the country, both in Northern and Southern Ireland.

"We wish," the resolution states, "to testify to the friendly relations which have always existed between all parties in this neighbourhood, we having never at any time received anything but the greatest kindness and consideration from our Roman Catholic fellow-men."—*Irish Times*, 8th April, 1922.

"Protests against the murders committed in Belfast were made yesterday by the Protestant com-

munity in Fermoy and the Irish Guild of the Church.
The following is the resolution passed by the
Protestants of Fermoy:

"We, the undersigned Protestants of Fermoy,
desire to express our utter horror and abhorrence of
the dastardly murders and outrages perpetrated on
our Catholic fellow-countrymen, women and children,
in the North of Ireland—murders which would disgrace the most uncivilised people in the world. We
also wish to warmly testify to the most cordial and
friendly relations which have always existed between
Catholics and Protestants in our town and district,
and to express the hope that some influential man in
Cork city will take immediate steps to convene a meeting of the Protestants of the city and county to make
a united protest.

"The list of names includes those representative
of the Church and commercial interests in Fermoy."—
Irish Times, 4th April, 1922.

―――――――

"At a largely atended meeting of the Protestants
of all denominations held in the Lecture Hall, Boyle,
on Tuesday, April 11th, 1922, under the chairmanship of Archdeacon Wagner, LL.D., a resolution was
unanimously passed expressing 'abhorrence and
detestation of the abominable crimes committed in
Belfast and elsewhere in our country, which we look
upon as a disgrace to our Christianity and common
humanity. Nothing can justify murder. The most
cordial and friendly relations always existed between
the Catholics and Protestants of this neighbourhood'."

―――――――

"It is the duty of the Protestant minority in the
South of Ireland to protest most strongly against the
action of their co-religionists in the North towards
their Catholic fellow-countrymen. In Southern Ireland, where the question of a man's religion never
enters into his relations with his fellow-men, and the

question of his politics but rarely, unless he is more than usually aggressive, it is difficult to understand why people should be murdered under most revolting circumstances in North-East Ulster because they do not hold the same religious and political opinions as their neighbours."—T. F. Newton-Brady, Crannagh, Nenagh, March 27th, 1922.—*Irish Times*, 29th March, 1922.

———

"As a Protestant living in the Co. Limerick, I have for many years lived in what is practically a wholly Roman Catholic community, and never once have I heard a word spoken against a Protestant on account of his religion. Personally I have never received anything but the greatest kindness from my Roman Catholic neighbours."—H. M. O'Grady, Castlegrade, Limerick, 25th March, 1922.—*Independent*, 28th March, 1922.

———

"Sir,—It seems quite unnecessary that anyone making any pretence to Christianity should say how much the horrible crimes that have been taking place in Belfast are abhorrent to him.

"I have lived all my life in Dublin and the South of Ireland, and some of my best and kindest friends are, and have been, Roman Catholics.

"To say that some Protestants, too, have been murdered does not alter the case. Two wrongs do not make a right.

"The Belfast people boast that they are progressive, industrious and enlightened, but they must hang their heads in bitter shame when they think of what has been happening in Belfast.—J. D. Cowen (Clerk in Holy Orders), Castletown Rectory, Nenagh, 28th March, 1922."—*Independent*, 30th March, 1922.

———

Mr. George Hutchinson, Lavitt's Quay, Cork, in a letter to the Press, says: "As a Protestant living among the Catholic people of Cork, from whom I have received nothing but the greatest kindness, I am ashamed at the acts of my co-religionists in the North. My business takes me to every town of any importance in Munster, and 95 p.c. of my customers are Roman Catholics.

" I have never lost a farthing's worth of business through being a Protestant. No matter what form of Government the Irish people set up, I am fully satisfied that the minority have absolutely nothing to be afraid of."—*Independent*, 4th April, 1922.

————

" SIR,—I notice in letters addressed to you from southern Protestants, there are none from West Roscommon condemning the wholesale murders of Catholics in Belfast. I am a Protestant living in the heart of a Catholic county, and I have always found my Catholic neighbours kind and obliging in every way. I am not the only Protestant in the district; there are several other families scattered here and there who can vouch for the friendly relations that exist between Catholics and Protestants in this part of the country. In fact, we could not run our farm if it were not for the neighbourly help from our Catholic friends.

" I wish to add my protest to the other Protestants, placed as I am, who have without fear or intimidation, signed a protest condemning the brutal murders of our own flesh and blood whose only crime is being Catholics. I sincerely pray that peace and harmony will be the result of the conference now being held between the heads of the Southern and Northern Parliaments.—Mrs. Monds, Knockroe, Castlerea.— *Independent*, 6th April, 1922.

————

" SIR,—A number of influential southern Protestants have asked me to organise a suitable meeting in Dublin to protest against the dreadful murders in the North of Ireland. A representative committee has been formed with a view to holding a national convention of Irish Protestants in the Mansion House to pass two resolutions: (1), condemning in the strongest manner the taking of human life in Belfast and elsewhere as a result of sectarian hatred; (2), declaring that southern Irish Protestants never suffer any religious intolerance of any kind from their Roman Catholic neighbours.

" In my opinion, the two resolutions are absolutely necessary. A national convention of Irish Protestants is the most suitable and effective means of exposing the national will. No politics of any kind should be introduced by any of the speakers at the convention. From personal interviews with some of the leading clerical and lay members of the various Protestant denominations in Dublin I can truthfully say that the proposed convention has their entire support. To-day the Lord Mayor of Dublin most willingly agreed to place the Mansion House at our disposal.

" I appeal to Protestants of every religious denomination in every county in Ireland to select without delay, and send in the names to me, their representatives at the convention. Due notice of the date of the convention will be published in the Press. —Yours, etc., Samuel Moore, K.C., Rathlin, Belgrave Road, Monkstown, April 6th, 1922."—*Irish Times*, 7th April, 1922.

" Mr. D. M. Rattray, Gortnaskehy, Ballybunion, writing to the secretary of the Listowel meeting explaining his absence owing to indisposition, and saying he was in full sympathy with its objects, says: ' I am now forty-four years residing in Co. Kerry. During that time no person has ever mentioned religion to me.

" ' I have found my Roman Catholic friends and neighbours the most kind, sympathetic, and obliging people that could be found in any country, and the happiest years of my life have been spent amongst them'."—*Independent*, 4th April, 1922.

" These dreadful sacrifices would not be tolerated amongst cannibals.

" I think it the duty of every southern Protestant to pay into a fund substantially for the relief of those destitute and homeless fellow-Catholics in the North. I will assist in any way I am wanted."—J. Johnston, Castlematrix, Rathkeale.—*Independent*, 3rd, April, 1922.

V.

ON THE FAILURE OF THE PACT.

CRAIG TO COLLINS.

" CABIN HILL, KNOCK,
" 25th April, 1922.

"DEAR MR. COLLINS,—I have received your telegram of the 22nd inst. The Government of Northern Ireland has conscientiously endeavoured to carry out the spirit and the letter of the Agreement. It is, therefore, with great surprise that I have read your statement that the Government of Northern Ireland is not fulfilling vital clauses of the Agreement. Taking the terms of that Agreement point by point:

" 1.—Northern Ireland has maintained peace with Southern Ireland, and has shown a spirit of conciliation in trying to co-operate with the Provisional Government in Education, Labour questions, and other matters tending to promote the interests of all classes in Ireland. It is with regret that we have learned of the determination of your Government to break off the joint railway inquiry, to which both our Covernments had given their consent. Your departments, as a whole, have not shown to the Government of Northern Ireland the courtesy and consideration which we have hoped for, and have taken action calculated to embarrass our administration, but we trust that this is merely due to lack of experience.

" 2.—Notwithstanding the undertaking of your Government, armed incursions into northern territory have continued. The Border Commission established by the Imperial Government was gradually fulfilling its purpose of restoring confidence on both sides of our frontier, but the recent violent interruption of its functions oy armed men who claim to be official members of the I.R.A. from Southern Ireland has a deplorable effect. The recent series of outrages committed by so-called Sinn Feiners against the property of Catholics in various districts in Northern Ireland is regarded by the latter as an effort to intimidate all those members of that faith who are anxious to work in harmony with our established Government.

" 3.—The disturbances in Belfast have, I regret to say, not been quelled, but the Government has been handicapped in suppressing crime by the terms of our Agreement. I had hoped that the establishment of a Catholic Constabulary Force, intended to protect Roman Catholic areas in Belfast, would have been in operation before this date. We have been waiting for the formation of the Roman Catholic Advisory Police Committee, but I have not yet received the names of your representatives for this committee. I am glad to learn, however, that there is now a probability that a Catholic Police Force in certain areas may shortly be established.

" 4.—The Courts which you were so anxious for us to establish, consisting of the Lord Chief Justice and the Lord Justice of Appeal, have been constituted, by special legislation. Moreover, in view of your representations regarding the partiality of the juries of Northern Ireland—a reflection which we entirely repudiate—we have arranged that all cases of violent death in Belfast shall be brought before the coroner without a jury.

" 5.—The Conciliation Committee referred to in Clause 5 of our Agreement is, I am glad to say, in operation. Suggestions have been made that they should inquire into past cases of murder, particularly into the case of the McMahons. Any efforts on their part to secure evidence at the inquest on this case, to be held shortly, or on any of the other recent outrages, will be welcomed by our Government. As I have already indicated, however, the rôle of this committee is not to supplant the judicial system of Northern Ireland, but to try to assist the authorities in putting an end to the terrible system of partisan vendetta, not only by helping to bring the criminals to justice and inculcating amongst all classes a determination not to tolerate crime by whomsoever committed, but also by securing amongst citizens of every religion a greater spirit of mutual forbearance.

" 6.—With regard to Article 6, the Government of Northern Ireland, realising the grave troubles with which the Provisional Government is confronted, has purposely refrained from adding to those difficulties by making adverse comments. They are willing to credit your Government with the intention of fulfilling your part of the Agreement when it is possible. In view of your remarks, however, it must be pointed out that grave outrages are still being committed within our borders by men claiming to be members of the I.R.A., that almost a score of persons who were kidnapped from our area are still illegally detained in Southern Ireland, and that the Border Commission, set up by the Imperial Government, has been brought into contempt and made ineffective. Moreover, although you have assured me that the boycott of Northern Ireland is absolutely contrary to the wishes of the Provisional Government, it is unfortunately true that, within the month which has elapsed since our Agreement, interference with our trade has been greater than in the whole previous period when the boycott was officially countenanced, and damage has been done to Northern Irish goods aggregating in value many hundreds of thousands of pounds. Our traders have shown great restraint, and our Government has urged them to adopt no methods of retaliation, but has advised them to apply in your courts for reparation and compensation, for which we understand your Government will assume ultimate responsibility.

" 7.—Article 7 does not yet arise.

" 8.—The Conciliation Committee will, I hope, be successful in carrying out Article 8 of our Agreement in regard to the return to their homes of expelled workers, but the difficulties of the situation are aggravated by the hostility of certain sections of the people in Southern Ireland towards the members of the R.I.C. who wish to return home on disbandment. I hope that St. Mary's Hall, Belfast, may be returned to its former owners as soon as they are in a position to guarantee that it will no longer be used for criminal purposes. We regret that you are not yet able to give any undertaking that the headquarters of the Orange institution in Dublin will be restored at an early date, although no suggestion has ever been made that it has been used for any illegal object. I believe that the seizure in Dublin of the Y.M.C.A. buildings and of the Freemasons' Hall, Molesworth Street, this week is opposed to the wishes of your Government, and is, therefore, an act of illegality of which we trust you will take immediate cognisance.

"9.—As regards the relief of unemployment in Belfast, the Minister of Labour of Northern Ireland has taken every step practicable to begin relief work, but the failure of the nominees of your Government to act on the Advisory Committee has caused considerable delay.

"10.—In regard to the release of prisoners, I made it quite clear at our conference in the Colonial Office that we could not acquiesce in a general release of all prisoners for offences committed prior to the date of Agreement, and that we could not countenance the liberation of those convicted of grave civil offences. In your list of nearly 170 prisoners, for whose release you make request, there is a very large proportion of criminals convicted of murder and other serious crimes. The Minister of Home Affairs of Northern Ireland is prepared to recommend to our Government—in accordance with the terms of our Agreement—the release of a number of persons convicted of technical offences of a so-called political character.

"11.—Finally, we would ask you most earnestly to remember the terms of Article 11 of our Agreement and to join with us in asking our peoples to exercise restraint in the interest of peace.

"Yours faithfully,

"JAMES CRAIG.

"Michael Collins, Esq., M.P.,
"City Hall, Dublin."

VI.

COLLINS TO CRAIG, 28th APRIL, 1922.

"The Right Hon. Sir James Craig,
     "Premier, Northern Ireland.

"Your letter of 25th inst. reached this office late last night. I did not see it until it had already appeared in the Press, consequently I wired you as follows:

> "'Your letter only reached my office late last night. Consider publication without reference to me the greatest want of courtesy. In view of this publication, I propose handing all further communications to the Press at the time of dispatch.'

"Your letter under acknowledgment so astonishes me by its assertions and general tone that I think it well to set out here my wire of 22nd April, to which I take it your letter is a reply:

> "'All here are agreed that it is impossible to make any further progress until vital clauses of the Agreement are fulfilled by you. Consider your attitude with regard to prisoners most unsatisfactory and entirely out of accord with letter and spirit of Agreement. Your failure to agree to investigation of cases under Clause 5 most unreasonable.'

"It will be observed that I have raised two main issues in this wire, namely:

     (a) Release of prisoners; and
     (b) Failure to agree to investigation under Clause 5.

"In your reply you carefully avoid these issues, and I must insist that it is no answer to these assertions to give a long list of vague and indefinite charges, backed up with a few dates and little evidence of any kind.

"You commence your letter by stating that your Government has conscientiously endeavoured to carry out the spirit and the letter of the Agreement. How can you maintain this assertion with regard to the points I make in my wire?

"Clause 10 of the Pact states that 'The two Governments shall, in cases agreed upon between the signatories, arrange for the release of political prisoners in prison for offences before the date hereof.' In pursuance of this Clause, I have caused the release of the Specials arrested at Clones, and furnished you, some weeks ago, with a list of 170 persons detained by your Government for purely political causes. So far, you have not released one single person on this list.

"Clause 5 of the Pact makes provision for a 'Committee to be set up in Belfast of equal members, Catholic and Protestant, with an independent chairman, preferably Catholic and Protestant alternating in successive weeks, to hear and investigate complaints as to intimidation, outrages, etc., such committee to have access to the heads of the Government. The local Press to be approached with a view to inserting only such reports of disturbances, etc. as shall have been considered and communicated by this committee.'

"What has your attitude been on this important matter? You have continually and emphatically refused my repeated request to you to get this committee established and functioning. On the 4th inst. you replied:

"'Your wire received, and I await the names you suggest for the two committees. In view of the pleasing fact that peace has reigned for over twenty-four hours, I consider it injudicious to go back either on the cases of Walsh, Spallen, M'Crory, and M'Kenna, or on that of the two constables shot earlier that day. The authorities are making every endeavour to bring the criminals to justice.'

" On the 5th I wired you:

" 'Your wire received; am consulting with regard to names to-day. All are satisfied that it is imperatively necessary to have inquiry into all cases, including the two constables. We believe continuation of peace and restoration of confidence depend on the inquiry. The conditions of the Agreement must apply rigidly from date of signing; otherwise they are valueless.'

" The same day you replied as follows

" 'Your telegram regarding inquiry received. I differ profoundly; a few days were required to establish the peaceful conditions now prevailing. I cannot consent to rake up past cases. Such action might cause fresh outburst of bitterness, which we are so anxious to avoid. I repeat that the authorities are endeavouring to bring the criminals to justice.'

" You will recollect that I further urged the necessity of the matter on the 5th inst. So much for this matter.

" Now, with regard to your letter of the 25th inst., it is such an astonishing accumulation of evasions and charges, supported by little or no data, that I can only conclude its *raison d'être* was for purely propaganda purposes—to be used *ad libitum* by the various journals of the great British Press combine, which is playing such an important part in the game of disunion and internal conflict in our common country.

" 1.—In Clause No. 1 of your letter you state that ' Northern Ireland has maintained peace with Southern Ireland and has shown a spirit of conciliation in trying to co-operate with the Provisional Government in Education, Labour questions and other matters tending to promote the interests of all classes in Ireland.' Whilst I fail to see what bearing these particular matters have on our Pact, at any rate your assertion that you have ' maintained peace ' and shown ' a spirit of conciliation ' with us is fully answered in this reply.

" I cannot see in what way my Government has b en discourteous to an authority in whose territory the members of the greatest Church in Christendom, which enjoys the protection of all civilised Governments, are harassed and persecuted in the most appalling fashion by armed mobs, who are apparently not interfered with in any way by your police or military. Under your jurisdiction—to name but a few instances—little Catholic school children playing in the streets, Catholic expectant mothers at the doors of their homes, a Catholic father and five members of his family in his own drawing-room, a Catholic woman in the porch of St. Matthew's Catholic Church, all in Belfast, have been foully and deliberately murdered in cold blood. You suggest that we lack experience. If this be the test of ' experienced government,' then we are happy to be called ' inexperienced.'

" (2).—You seek to make capital out of certain alleged happenings with respect to the Border Commission. I confess I am astonished at your mentioning the Border Commission in view of the extraordinary attitude your authorities have adopted with regard to it. Let me refresh your memory on the matter.

" The regulations creating the Commission were issued on the 17th February. According to these regulations the personnel of the Commission was to be formed thus:

" ' Two officers of the Dublin Garrison will work on the North side of the border in company with two officers of the Special Constabulary detailed by the Northern Government. Similarly, two officers of the Dublin Garrison will work on the South side of the border in company with two officers nominated by the Provisional Government.'

" The British Government and our Government in due course appointed our representatives. Up to date you have only appointed one—viz., District Inspector King—and even him you have not vested with full powers. On 24th February, District Inspector King attended two meetings of the Joint Commission and informed the Commission that he had no authority whatever from the Northern Government to give effect to any of the Commission's findings, and that he did not even forward reports of the proceedings to the Northern Government. At a very early stage in the proceedings—to be exact, the 24th. February—the Provisional Government undertook to give immediate effect to any unanimous decision of the Commission.

"On the 6th March, your representative, Lieut.-Colonel Vernon, who had proceeded to Belfast to represent the views of the Southern representatives with reference to the prisoners still detained by the North, stated that he was referred to Paragraph 6 of his instructions, which ' could not be modified.' The paragraph referred to read as follows:

" ' You will, however, refrain from entering into any discussion affecting questions of policy, which are within the competence of the Northern Government, or affecting the administration of justice dealing with the cases of men awaiting trial.'

" Again, at a meeting of the Commission on the Monaghan-Tyrone Border on the 10th March, the official report states:

" ' There was no reply from the Northern Government re the request of the Joint Commission to have the Northern representative placed in a position similar to that occupied by the representative for the Provisional Government.'

" Lieut.-Colonel Montagu Bates' official report of the 14th inst. contains this significant paragraph:

" ' Every opportunity of publishing exaggerated reports is made use of by Press representatives of the Northern papers. As previously reported, these exaggerated reports do an immense amount of harm amongst the local inhabitants near the Border and elsewhere.'

" The white and blue flag of the Commission has

always been respected by us, but see Paragraph 4 of Lieut.-Colonel Montagu Bates" report for the following:

"'On passing through Aughnacloy on the return journey yesterday, we were given to understand by a Head-Constable of the Special Constabulary that they had orders to fire at sight on any car flying the blue and white flag.'

"I agree with you that 'the Border Commission was gradually fulfilling its purpose of restoring peace on both sides' of the Border, but, in view of the facts recorded above, it is obviously absurd to blame us for any violent interruption of its functions.

"Your entire letter has apparently been drafted with a view to keeping attention off the daily practice of atrocities and murders which continue uninterrupted in the seat of your Government. There is not space here to detail all the abominations that have taken place in Belfast since the signing of our Pact, and I quite understand your desire to draw the attention of civilisation away from them. This much, though, I must say—the ink on our Pact was scarcely dry when, on the 1st inst., loads of armed Specials, uniformed and un-uniformed, in Crossley tenders and whippet cars, invaded, during Curfew hours, Stanhope Street and Arnon Street, where 90 per cent. of the inhabitants are Catholics, and entered the houses of many of the Catholics. The result of this armed incursion was that four Catholics, one of whom was an old man, and three of whom fought on the British side in the European War, were tortured and murdered in their beds, and in the presence of their wives. You refer to an alleged 'cowardly ambuscade.' As you appear to be confident as to the identity of the culprits in this case, I trust you will assist the Provisional Government in bringing them to justice.

"You make the extraordinary statement that certain Catholics have destroyed Catholic property in your area. Is this statement also intended to assist the big British Press combine which has arranged to do propaganda for you? If not, I trust you will furnish us with particulars of these remarkable Catholics.

"Your statement that you have not yet received the names of our representatives of your Catholic Advisory Police Committee is contrary to the facts. The names were in your hands on the date you dictated your letter. Let me state here that I cannot take any part in assisting you in the formation of a police force for your area until I am clearly convinced that the lives of its members will be safe, and that it will be able to do something to restore law and order in Belfast. In order to achieve this salutary purpose, it seems to me that the committee should at once proceed under Clause 5 of the Pact to investigate the attempted assassination of Constable Moriarty, a Catholic member of the Belfast Constabulary, in the porch of St. Matthew's Church last Sunday evening.

"I note with satisfaction your recent actions with regard to your Courts.

"The Conciliation Committee is, I presume, the Investigation Committee referred to in Clause 5 of our Agreement. I understand you have not facilitated them in any way. On the contrary, they have been unable to obtain direct access to the heads of your Government, and this, notwithstanding the fact that they have been meeting since April 12th, and that outrages and intimidation on an increasing scale are taking place daily in Belfast.

"No one, to my knowledge, suggested that they should inquire into the McMahon massacre, but I have insisted that they should inquire into all outrages since the signing of the Pact on March 30th. As the McMahon massacre was perpetrated before March 30th, your allusion to this is a deliberate attempt to confuse the issue. You have persistently refused that they should inquire into the Stanhope Street and Arnon Street atrocities, already referred to.

"The reinstitution of the boycott by certain unofficial and irregular parties is unfortunate; but I am convinced that if you had co-operated, as you undertook under Clause 11 of the Pact, you would not have grounds for a complaint of this nature against the people of Ireland.

"I am determined that the awful conditions that have been existing in your area since the devolution of certain powers on you will not be tolerated in the rest of Ireland, but if you want quick results in this respect the best way to get them is by protecting the lives and property of the 25 per cent. of the population of Belfast which is being gradually exterminated.

"Many members of the R.I.C. at present in Belfast are anxiously awaiting the termination of their contract with you in order to enjoy security elsewhere in Ireland and avoid the fate intended for Constable Moriarty and meted out to other constables by people under your jurisdiction.

"Repeated demands have been made to you for possession of St. Mary's Hall—one no later than Monday last to Sir Dawson Bates—and it has been pointed out to your Minister of Home Affairs that it is urgently required for charitable purposes, and for a shelter for people burnt out of their homes in Catholic streets in North Belfast and at present herded together in a pitiable way—men, women and children—in wooden huts on waste grounds in your city, and without any conveniences whatever. You may rest assured that citizens of Orange proclivities, and their property, will never be refused ample protection by us.

"As arranged in London, I have handed you the list of names of persons on the White Cross Committee in Belfast who are to act on the Advisory Committee set up by your Minister of Labour.

"I have already referred to the question of the prisoners. There is one point, however, in your letter on this matter on which I would thank you for an explanation. You say: ' In your list of nearly 170 prisoners, for whose release you make request, there is a very large proportion of criminals convicted of murder and other serious crimes.' Have your courts convicted more than three persons on that list of murder, and are not these obviously political cases?

"As to Clause 11.—I have always shown a willingness and desire, as you well know, to meet you as far as possible on every possible ground, but I must say I have not met with anything like a similar spirit of co-operation from either yourself or your colleagues. On the contrary, you appear to have shown at best a reluctance to make even the slightest effort to interfere with the unrestrained violence of the savage mobs under your jurisdiction. Of course, I make all allowance for your inability to deal effectively with these barbarians in your midst, but. I must say the recent utterances of your colleagues in Belfast are anything but helpful towards peace, and, in my opinion, constitute a very grave breach of this Clause 11.

" Since the Pact the following awful list of murder, arson and general crime has been committed in the very centre of your seat of Government:

From 1st April, 1922, to date:

Catholics killed 24
Catholics wounded   41
Attempted murders of Catholics   29
No. of (R.C.) houses burned and looted   ... 75
No. of (R.C.) families homeless   89
No. of (R.C.) persons homeless   400
No. of (R.C.) houses bombed   5
No. of Protestants killed 11
No. of Protestants wounded   34
No. of Protestant houses looted and burned ... 11

" Two of the Protestants killed—Matthew Carmichael and Johnston (26, Moyola Street, and 20, Harrison Street)—were shot dead in an entirely Orange locality, and were mistaken for Catholics. The Protestant premises were destroyed by loyalists during the outbreak at Marrowbone (at Easter). No record of any Protestant families homeless, as there are hundreds of houses from which Catholics have been evicted for them to occupy.

" This is, you will admit, I am sure, an appalling record of crime to happen in the chief city of any Government which calls itself civilised, especially after having entered into an honourable agreement with us in which you undertook to restore ordered conditions in your area.

"I would suggest to you that it would be much better for the peace of your area and the general welfare of our country if you devoted your energies in co-operation with us, in the true spirit of the Agreement, towards establishing civilised conditions in Belfast.

"MICHEAL O COILEAIN."

VII.

REPLY TO THE LONDON *SPECTATOR'S* MISLEADING ARTICLE.

THE Belfast Catholic Protection Committee issued the following statement, 12th May, 1922 :

"An article taken from the *Spectator* has appeared in the issue of Belfast *Evening Telegraph* of 6th May. This article, amongst other things, referred to the reign of violence in Ulster, and particularly in Belfast. The statements in the article which refer to Belfast are untrue, and patently propagandist in tone. But there is one part of a sentence which reads as follows: 'The monstrous charge that Roman Catholics, as such in Belfast, have been subjected to savage persecution.'

"The presence of these words in the article gives the idea that it was, perhaps, written without knowledge of the real facts, and that if these were supplied to the writer he would probably be horrified to find that a savage persecution is being directed against Catholics in Belfast, as such.

"It is stated in the article that 'all the evidence shows first that the original trouble came from the Sinn Fein gunmen imported into Belfast.'

"We wonder what the evidence is. It has never been made public yet, to our knowledge. This excuse has been made in the Orange Press of Belfast to justify murder, and as an incitement to arson and murder; but there was no evidence produced.

As a matter of fact the only Sinn Feiners imported into Belfast were those imported into Crumlin Road Jail by the British Government, and these were not in a position to offend.

" ' Sinn Fein ' gunmen could not be served up as an excuse for the expulsion of the Catholic workmen from the shipyards in 1912. Neither could they be made to serve as an excuse for the expulsion of Catholics from the shipyards in 1886.

" At both these times, as in 1920, the Catholic workers, as such, were savagely attacked and beaten, some driven into the water and pelted when swimming to safety. One was drowned under particularly brutal circumstances in 1886: a boy named Curran, aged seventeen years. In 1872 and 1864 persecution of Catholics occurred without the incitement of Sinn Fein gunmen.

" Belfast Catholics never at any period enjoyed tolerance. Religious bigotry is always present and it blazes into savage persecution at times when it is deemed necessary by interested politicians to use it as a political weapon.

" We further read that ' the boycott of Roman Catholic workers in the shipyards was put into practice, not because these workers were Roman Catholics, but because they would not disavow the Sinn Fein policy of murder.'

" Does the writer mean by this that an alternative was given to Catholics before being expelled?

" Here is the way the boycott was ' put into practice ': Crowds of thousands of Protestants, armed with sledges, rivets and revolvers, and bars of iron attacked the Catholics on a given day at a given signal, beat those whom they caught so savagely that some died from the effects, hunted them for their lives from their work like wild beasts: some had to swim across the docks for safety.

" Over 4000 were thus treated, of whom 1,500 were ex-soldiers who had served in France. Not one solitary individual was given the alternative. The only question asked that day was: ' Are you a Papish?' Later on, when it was found that religious bigotry had gone too far, and had developed into savage persecution by denying fundamental rights to fellow-human beings to earn their bread, the excuse of the alternative was made.

" Over a month after all the Catholics, without exception, had been driven violently from work, the alternative was invented to make politics an excuse.

" Ten thousand men are in receipt of White Cross relief; 4000 of these were driven from the shipyards; 6000 were driven from foundries, mills, factories and other works. One thousand Catholic women are in receipt of this relief. The dependents of these number about 30,000.

" To say that any of these 11,000 people were offered an alternative is a lie. To say that they were Sinn Feiners is a lie. They were denied the right to work because they were Catholics.

" Upwards of 500 Catholic shopkeepers have had their shops burned, looted and wrecked, and their means of livelihood taken from them.

" Hundreds of Catholic families in Belfast alone have been rendered homeless by being burned and looted and wrecked.

" Protestants married to Catholics have been hounded from their work; have been bombed and shot and driven from their homes.

" Catholic R.I.C. men and R.I.C. pensioners have had their houses bombed and have been driven from their homes as well.

" Catholic women have been deliberately murdered in cold blood by murder gangs—amongst them expectant mothers.

" Catholic children of mixed marriages have been killed by murder gangs.

" Catholic ex-soldiers have been driven from the hospitals in which they were patients.

" Foreigners in Belfast belonging to Catholic nations have had their premises wrecked and have been assaulted and shot.

" Catholic groups of children at play have been bombed with horrible results.

" Catholic congregations attending Divine Service have been attacked with fatal results.

"Catholic churches and convents and parochial houses have also been attacked and partly burned.

"Catholic clergymen have been insulted and shot at.

"All the evidence goes to show that the original trouble is not political by any means, but religious. To be a Catholic is a crime punishable by death in Belfast. Age and sex have not been spared, from the babe unborn to the octogenarian.

"Regarding the fate of the McMahon family, even the Protestant leaders of the North had not the hardihood to suggest what this article does, that this unfortunate family were murdered by ' Sinn Fein gunmen.'

"The residence of the McMahons is not a quarter of a mile from Glenravel Street Police Barracks. On the night this family were murdered their door was battered in with a sledge-hammer. A crowd of murderers leisurely accomplished their fell work during the Curfew hours, when none but members of the Crown Forces dare go abroad. The noise made was heard over a wide area, and yet no one came on the scene until all was over and the murderers escaped, in spite of the fact that a number of Special Constables must have been on duty on Antrim Road.

"The Northern Government offered £1000 reward for the perpetrators of the deed, but it has not yet been claimed.

"The evidence that the Protestant leaders might have put forward was similar to the type of evidence that attributed the murder of Lord Mayor MacCurtain of Cork to 'Sinn Fein gunmen,' that attributed the burning of Cork city to Sinn Fein incendiaries or that attributed the murders of the Mayor and ex-Mayor of Limerick to 'Sinn Fein gunmen,' etc.; and as such they, not being fools, did not bring it forward, for evidence of this type is now 'played out,' even for propaganda purposes."

INDEX.

211

Orange Aggression:

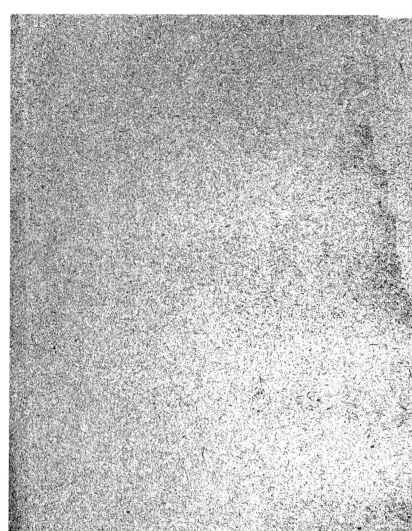